spin, the water will be sprayed throughout the works. Repeat with cold water to rinse.

Chip Rowe, Washington DC, USA

GLUE CDs together back-to-back. Play one side, then flip it over and play the other, just like your old vinyl records.

Warren Wilson, Chifley, Australia

KEEP all your CDs In the wrong cases. If a burglar steals them, at least he'll

have the unenviable task of sorting them out before he can sell them to his 'fence'.

P. Legg, Lyndhurst

RADIOHEAD. Make £150 million, then give away an album free saying you are against the business side of the music industry.

Colin, e-mail

DON'T waste your money on Christmas singles this year. Come December, just listen to normal singles and shake some sleigh bells towards the end of the record.

E. Park, Portsmouth

INDIE bands. When you finally get to appear on television after years and years of playing the gig circuit, sending demos to radio stations and traipsing around every record company in London, don't forget to stand there looking miserable, as if it's the last

place in the world you want to be.

C. Sanders, Kentucky

RATHER than spending a fortune on new gramophone records, try playing old ones at different speeds. Invariably a new 'sound' emerges, with the singer's voice changing somewhat in pitch.

B. West, Blackheath

CONVINCE neighbours you are a multi-instrumentalist by having a guitar, piano, saxophone, some drums, speakers and microphones and lots of recording equipment delivered to your house. Then open all your windows and play something by Mike Oldfield very loudly.

Eric Underpants, Lupset

CAN'T remember the artist or title of a song stuck in your head? Simply record and release the song and wait to be sued for breach of copyright. The information you need will be on the writ.

Simon Sandall, Brisbane

Compiled and Edited by
Graham Dury, Davey Jones and Simon Thorp

Designed by
Wayne Gamble

Production Manager
Stevie Glover

Viz would like to thank all the readers over the years who have
sent in their Top Tips. Thanks.

Tops Tips appear every five weeks in Viz Comic. Submit a Top
Tip by post: **Viz Comic, PO Box 656, North Shields, NE30 4XX**,
e-mail: **toptips@viz.co.uk**, tweet: **twitter.com/viztoptips**, or via
the website: **www.viz.co.uk**

First published 2010 by Dennis Publishing Ltd., 30 Cleveland
Street, London W1T 4JD. Distributed by Pan Macmillan Ltd.

ISBN 978-1-907232-83-1

A CIP catalogue record, whatever that is, for this book is available
from the British Library.

Printed in the United Kingdom.

www.viz.co.uk

MARRIED couples. Find out where you live in relation to other buildings in the neighbourhood by driving to a nearby hill while your 'other half' lets off an emergency flare from a bedroom window.

R. Worsnop,
Chesterfield

BRIGHTEN up boring snooker on TV by purchasing a sucker-tipped dart gun and trying to hit the players on the bottom as they bend down over the table.

A. Foster,
Bury

JELLY from pork pies, once warmed up, can be easily spread with a brush and is an economical substitute for varnish on doors, cupboards and skirting boards.

Lee and Dogs,
Cleveland

RE-SPRAYING your car? Cover it with clingfilm first. If you don't like the new colour, simply peel it off and start again!

Denise Jordan,
Petts Wood

A GLASS full of Marmite topped with shaving foam makes a quite convincing pint of Guinness, and has the advantage of tasting nicer.

Barry Carlisle,
Froam

THICKEN up runny low-fat yoghurt by stirring in a spoonful of lard.

P. Raker,
Chatham

KEEP Sunday Special campaigners. Wear a large yellow hat at all times. Shopkeepers can then put up signs saying 'Sorry -we do not serve people with yellow hats on Sundays'. That way everyone will be happy.

G. Widdle,
Swansea

KEEP a foot pump next to the brake pedal in your car, and connect it to an inflatable paddling pool folded on your lap. If you are about to crash, pump rapidly and the inflated pool will cushion you from injury.

J. Thompson,
Prestwick

IT IS easier to sharpen the end of a worm into a point using a pencil sharpener if you freeze it first.

K. Newton, Burnley

ATTEMPT your own corrective laser eye surgery by removing the back of your CD player and then staring into it whilst it is switched on.

P.S.,
Leicester

FELLAS. Keep a pile of bricks together with the names and addresses of all your ex-girlfriends next to the telly so that if your lottery numbers come up you can go straight round their houses and put their windows in. It will serve them right for dishing the

dirt on you in the papers later that week, which they're bound to do.

B. Labone,
Everton

PRETEND you don't live in Tottenham by walking around Tottenham with an A to Z guide asking people for directions.

Simone Glover,
Tottenham

SWEDES make ideal (if not slightly small) turnips for people who don't like turnips.

Mr Vic Ground,
Stoke on Trent

SNIP the tails off several hundred small tadpoles using nail scissors to make a tasty (and cheap) caviar substitute.

D. Tanby,
Formby

OFFICE workers. Half a ball of Edam cheese makes a handy desk top 'pen cushion', and can be nibbled if you become peckish between meals.

A. Madeupname,
Ficticiousplace

POKER players. An old scrubbing brush upturned on the table is ideal for standing your cards upright in, leaving both hands free to pour whisky, light cigarettes, adjust your hat, etc.

B.C. Smith,
Edinburgh

"You'll like Tip... Not a Lot!"

WITH Paul Daniels

PREPARE baby turtles for their hectic life at sea by placing them in a washing machine. Add salt instead of soap and you have the perfect 'ocean simulator'.
S.R., Dundee

SAVE petrol by pushing your car to your destination. Invariably passers-by will think you've broken down and help.
S. Pate, Glasgow

SCOTCH perverts. Attach your kilt to your belt with curtain rings. You can then expose yourself quickly and effortlessly by simply drawing your kilt to and fro. A simple draw string mechanism, available from all curtain shops, can be added later if required.
S. Cheesecake, Rotherham

PASS yourself off as Welsh by putting coal dust behind your fingernails and talking gibberish all the time, stopping occasionally to sing loudly, or set fire to someone else's house.
Mr P. Lilburn, Rotherham

TRAIN travellers. A simple box of Black Magic chocolates makes a convincing substitute for those who cannot afford the latest 'lap-top' computer. Open it on the table in front of you, and pretend to 'type' an important business memo on the chocolates, whilst looking studiously at the inside of the lid. If you feel peckish, simply eat one of your 'keys'.
B.O., Norwich

AVOID jetlag on foreign trips by simply taking an earlier flight, thus arriving fully refreshed and on time.
Sgt. R. J. Crowe, 662 Squadron, Germany

NORMAL-sized Mars bars make ideal king-sized Mars bars for dwarfs, as well as fun-sized ones for giants.
T. Dell, Southampton

MODERNISE old fashioned flared trousers by removing a triangle of cloth from the bottom of each leg and sewing the gap closed. The spare triangles can then be attached to a length of string and used as bunting to decorate your street on party occasions such as royal anniversaries, weddings etc. Sombre bunting from black trousers could be used for the Queen Mother's funeral.
J. Black, Fulchester

LOOK 'hard' on train journeys by saving up all your empty beer cans for a month and then lining them up on the table in front of you.
Tugger Trotman, Wirral

MUFFLE the sound of your iPod to prevent it annoying others by placing a tea bag between your headphones and each ear.
A. Asda,
Castleford

ATTACH a tag bearing your name and address to your house keys. If they are lost, whoever finds them can then re-turn them to you. On the back of the tag list the times when your house is empty, so that they'll be sure to catch you when they call.
P. Pegley,
Hammersmith

ROD HULL'S ROOF TOP TIPS

DON'T risk drowning next time you travel by boat. Simply wear a pair of bicycle clips and fill your trousers with ping-pong balls.
A. Clayton,
Glasgow

SCUBA divers. A deflated wheel barrow inner-tube worn around the neck makes a stylish polo neck for your wet suit.
C. Boulton,
Derby

HOLD an impromptu reunion of all your relatives, most of whom you haven't seen for years by simply winning the lottery. Hey presto! Just watch the freeloading fuckers turn up by the car load, all wanting a slice of the action.

Leighton Calvert,
Edinburgh

WHEN they die, embalm household pets and seal them in plastic to make perfect draught excluders. It's nice to know that your much-loved pets are still with you around the house, helping to keep you warm on cold winter nights.

Mrs L. Eptons,
Birkenhead

POLO mints scattered around the floor will deter mice from entering the room. They have a strong aversion to peppermint.

L. Haworth,
Crumpsall

STUCK for plates on your picnic? Simply remove your car wheel trims. Voila! Ideal for sausage rolls and chicken breasts.

Ma Wazzer,
Liverpool

POSTAGE stamps make ideal temporary repairs for punctured tyres or inner tubes.

Mr M. Haworth,
Crumpsall

I SLEEP with my house key under my tongue, and I never suffer from cramp.

Mrs T. Yorath,
Carlisle

CLAP your hands whilst having a shower. This will help to spray the water in all directions.

Chris Elvin,
Japan

MUMS. Stop children putting their elbows on the table at meal times by covering the table top in cement, and sprinkling it with broken glass. Leave small circles clear for plates, cups etc.

R.C. ,
Ashington

DON'T throw away that left-over paint. Turn your garden into a helicopter landing pad by painting a large 'H' in the middle of the lawn, using white emulsion and a roller.

Paul Sweeney,
Kirkham

FIND your way to the toilet in the dark by tying a length of string from the toilet bowl to the toilet door handle. Simply straddle the string and slide the cleft of your buttocks along it until you feel the toilet seat touch your genitals. Simple.

S. Jeames,
Brighton

POLO mints make excellent 'spearmint washers' for drinking water taps, and after a drink of water they leave your breath minty fresh.

Raminder Plinth,
Ilford

SAVE money on batteries by making your own novel doorbell. Simply thread some empty beer cans on a piece of string and hang them from the front door. Visitors can rattle them to attract your attention.

A. Soreskin,
Swindon

9

TOMORROW'S TIPS

WITH

JAMES BURKE

SAVE on expensive loo roll by taking a gripping book to the toilet with you. You'll become so engrossed that whatever there was to wipe will have dried up by the time you put the book down.

M. Armalade, Teddington Lock

KEEP a roll of Sellotape handy in the bathroom to stick back any unused pieces of toilet tissue which you pull off the roll by mistake.

D. Page, Burnley

WHEN buying toilet tissue I always unwind each roll carefully and number the sheets individually using a Biro or felt-tipped pen.

Mrs Howard, Bingley

ATTACH a 'bayonet' to your TV remote control by taping a fork to it. This way you can keep control of the television whilst eating TV snacks.

A. Cowie, Duns

WEAR a miner's helmet in bed. Not only does it provide emergency light in the event of power failure, but it also protects against unexpected falls of plaster from the ceiling.

Mr M. G. Midget, Harwich

APPLY red nail varnish to fingernails before clipping them. The red nails will be much easier to spot on your bathroom carpet, (unless you have a red carpet, in which case a contrasting varnish should be selected).

K. Parks, North Chittagong

AFTER dinner, save the expense of a coffee percolator by simply putting fresh coffee in a pot and adding hot water. Then ask guests to wear an old stocking over their head whilst drinking to stop any bits getting in their mouth. The denier of the stocking can be changed according to whether you are drinking espresso or coarse ground.

P Cotton, Wells, Somerset

NEXT time you're at the seaside try turning your greenhouse upside down and fitting an outboard motor. The kids will be kept occupied for hours watching the fascinating underwater flora and colourful fish.

M. Thresher, Bristol

SMALL lengths of rubber pipe make ideal 'skin tight body suits' for worms. Roll the worm in talcum powder first to ensure a comfortable fit.

K. Newton, Burnley

PENSIONERS. DON'T forget to retire to bed before 8.00pm so that you can get up tomorrow at the crack of dawn and go and collect your morning paper while anyone with any sense is still sound asleep in bed.

D. Lynch, Quatar

A TEASPOON placed in a glass on the back seat of your car makes a handy audible gauge for road bump severity.

R. Crabb, Nantwich

GALAXY Minstrels joined together by a cocktail stick would make a perfect set of dumbells for a squirrel if they were bigger. And heavier.

Leigh Lovelady, Tamworth

JOIN together hundreds of paper clips to make yourself an attractive 'chain mail' tank top, ideal for a 'knight' out!

Paul Harvey, Ash Green

WATER-filled fire extinguishers make ideal 'oxygen cylinders' for dolphins should they be taken out of the water at any time, for transportation etc.

P. Field, Sussex

STAND your cooker on an old tea chest. This prevents young children reaching the hot areas, and provides useful storage space for kitchen cleaning equipment, Domestos etc.

Curly Lox, Glastonbury

LIGHTHOUSE keepers. Amuse ships' captains by painting the walls of your lighthouse pink and the top purple, then standing on the top, getting the foghorn to go "Ugh! Ugh!" while you throw buckets of wallpaper paste up in the air.

Ian Finlay, Jedburgh

HIGH blood pressure sufferers. Simply cut yourself and bleed for a while, thus reducing the pressure in your veins.

N. Rodwell, Herne Bay

around your waist with the four bands hanging from it, with a crocodile clip stuck to the bottom of each one.

C. Gateau, Hebden Bridge

FELLAS. Why waste money on expensive '0898' phone numbers. Just phone your local department store, tell them its your wife's birthday, and ask them to describe their latest selection of ladies' lingerie (while you masturbate furiously).

A. Jax, Wolverhampton

WHEEL clamps can probably be used to secure dustbin lids to the ground, thus preventing them from being stolen, or blown away on windy nights.

J.B., Timperley

SAVE yourself the trouble of re-potting houseplants by putting them in a big enough pot in the first place.

P. Manderville, Marlborough

SMELL gas? Locate the suspected leak by striking an ordinary match in every room in the house until a loud explosion reveals the source of the escaping gas.

N. Burke, Manchester

CONVINCE friends you've joined the Socialist Workers' Party by becoming unsociable, giving up work, and standing on street corners ranting away on subjects about which you know very little.

Karl Lyall, Carlisle

PUT your microwave oven on a shelf inside your freezer. That way it will be able to freeze food as well as heat it up.

Mrs D. Pillage, Burton-on-Trent

CONVINCE your postman that you are more popular than you actually are by sending yourself several hundred Christmas cards each year.

T. James, Huddersfield

USE only economy packs of toilet roll instead of expensive 'luxury' tissue. You'll find that your fingers invariably go through both. But the money you save buying cheaper paper can then be spent on a bar of soap to clean them with.

Mrs E. Sharp, Grunty Fen

GIRLS. A saucy 'rubber fetish'-style suspender belt can be made from an old bicycle inner tube and four elastic bands. Slip the tube

TRY USING Cola cubes instead of Oxo cubes. Not only will it put the fizz back into tired old recipes, it also considerably reduces the risk of BSE.

Daisy Duke, Hazzard

GAME show enthusiasts. By taking a potato waffle, standing it on its side and placing an insect in each hole, you can recreate your own miniature 'Celebrity Squares'. It would probably be more exciting than the show itself was.

E. Grant, Newcastle

JIM TIPPED IT FOR ME

MAKE the postman think you have been sick by opening the door with diced carrots, rice pudding and parmesan cheese smeared down the front of your shirt.
Patrick Thistle, Partick Thistle

INTERNET users. Save yourself a lot of time and money by simply ringing a public call box and waiting for some sad bastard to walk by with nothing better to do than answer it.
S. Hope, Long Eaton

A BUCKET of water hung in a tree is an ideal nesting place for migrating sea birds.
H. Lovatt, Reading

LOOK like a super-fit body builder by buying a vest that's too small for you and walking around pretending that you've got a roll of carpet under each arm.
Hapag Lloyd, Runcorn

SAVE constant wear and tear on door hinges by only opening doors a little bit, and then squeezing through the gap.
Dino, Eastleigh

GRANDAD'S old army helmet, painted green and placed on a roller skate makes an ideal play-mate for lonely pet tortoises.
Phil W., Liverpool

CLAUSTROPHOBICS. Reduce the risk of panic when entering a lift by looking through the wrong end of a pair of binoculars.
T. R. Ilbey, Hattington

INCREASE the life of your carpets by rolling them up and keeping them in the garage.
A. Allied, South Wales

INCREASE blind people's electricity bills by switching all their lights on when their guide dog isn't looking.
P. F., Stanley

CONVERT potatoes into convincing hand grenades by cover-ing them in shoe segs and painting them green.
D.B., Harwich

AT party time put food colouring in guests' drinks, a different colour for each guest. Not only will the colours brighten up your party, but if anyone urinates on the bathroom floor you'll know who it was.
Innes Reid, Bangor

12

ALWAYS STROKE tigers and lions in the direction in which their fur lies. Never stroke against the nap of the fur, as it can make them extremely angry.
Chorlton Cumhardy,
Kenilworth

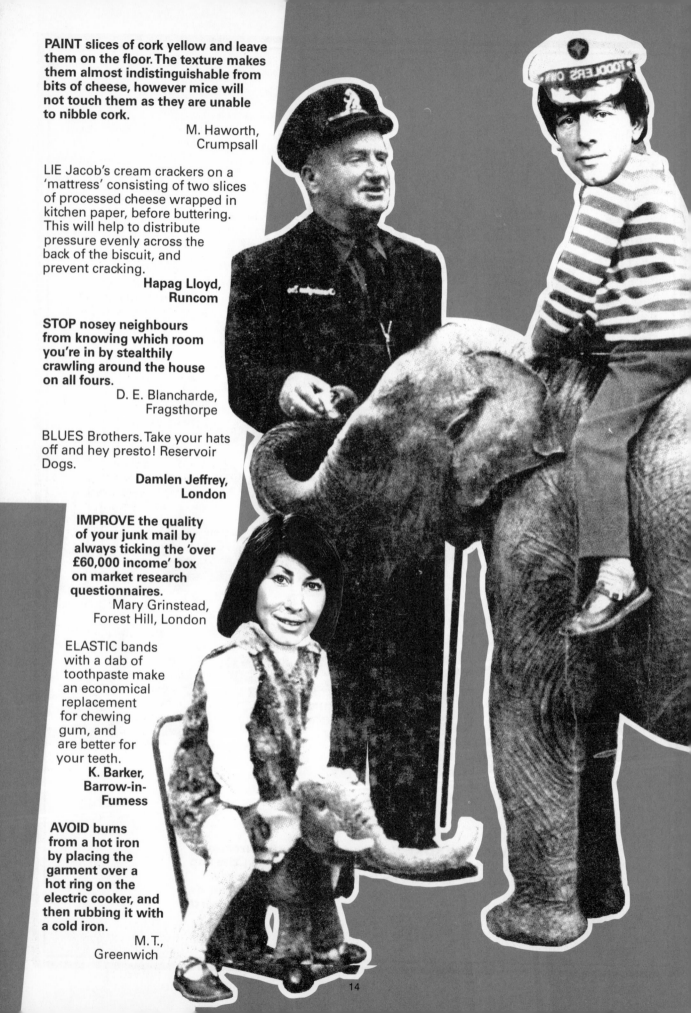

PAINT slices of cork yellow and leave them on the floor. The texture makes them almost indistinguishable from bits of cheese, however mice will not touch them as they are unable to nibble cork.

M. Haworth,
Crumpsall

LIE Jacob's cream crackers on a 'mattress' consisting of two slices of processed cheese wrapped in kitchen paper, before buttering. This will help to distribute pressure evenly across the back of the biscuit, and prevent cracking.

**Hapag Lloyd,
Runcom**

STOP nosey neighbours from knowing which room you're in by stealthily crawling around the house on all fours.

D. E. Blancharde,
Fragsthorpe

BLUES Brothers. Take your hats off and hey presto! Reservoir Dogs.

**Damlen Jeffrey,
London**

IMPROVE the quality of your junk mail by always ticking the 'over £60,000 income' box on market research questionnaires.

Mary Grinstead,
Forest Hill, London

ELASTIC bands with a dab of toothpaste make an economical replacement for chewing gum, and are better for your teeth.

**K. Barker,
Barrow-in-
Fumess**

AVOID burns from a hot iron by placing the garment over a hot ring on the electric cooker, and then rubbing it with a cold iron.

M. T.,
Greenwich

WITH THE

Blue Peter Shitting Elephant

KEEP your insurance company on their toes by ringing them to say that your roof has just blown off in a storm, then calling back ten minutes later to say that you were mistaken.
I. Battenburg, Walsall

KEEP your washing machine clean when out of use by leaving it running on the 'hot whites wash' setting.
T. Foster, Alton

DON'T answer your front door. It could be burglars.
Mr F. Corsair, Bridgnorth

CUT along one edge of a tea bag and empty out the contents to make an ideal After Eight mint cosy.
A. Asda, Castleford

A SHEET of thick plywood cut into small cubes makes ideal 'Liquorice Allsorts' for sweet-toothed woodpeckers or woodworms.
K. Warton, Stamford

AVOID dirty finger marks around light switches by fixing an ordinary bathroom soap dish and a glass holder by the side of each switch. Guests can then use the soap, and water from the glass, to wash their hands before touching the switch. Oh, and you'll need a small towel rail too.
Mrs. M. Head, Willenhall

FLATULENT people. When you go out always keep a 'Whoopee cushion' in your back pocket. As you're about to fart, simply sit down, then produce the cushion from behind you whilst laughing childishly.
C. Ground, Nottingham

BOOK liposuction sessions as close to Christmas as possible. This way money can be saved by using your excess fat to baste the turkey and roast the potatoes.
A. L., Ardley

WHO needs a dishwasher? Simply arrange your dirty dishes on your next door neighbour's roof-rack the next time he goes to the car wash.
R. Hughes, Mid Glamorgan

USE talcum powder on cakes instead of icing sugar. It's a lot cheaper, and much kinder to teeth.
Miss J. Holland, Southfields

AMAZE your neighbours by tightrope walking across your clothes line without the use of a safety net. Simply thread the clothes line through short sections of hosepipes glued to the bottom of your shoes. Providing your shoelaces are tied tightly, falling off is impossible.
M. Board, Romney

NEXT time you decorate, put wallpaper up with Blu-Tac. It's much less messy and expensive wallpaper can then be taken with you when you move house.
E. McAndrews, Didsbury

ONE or two days before moving house, place your goldfish bowl in the ice-making compartment of your refrigerator. When the time comes to move you will find that your fish can be transported in a car or van with no danger of spillage.

Mr D. A. Roberts,
Hillingdon

BUY a television set exactly like your neighbour's. Then annoy them by standing outside their window and changing their channel using your identical remote control.

High Drake,
Portsmouth

LIVE every day as if it were your last by converting your bedroom into an intensive care ward, inserting pipes into your nose and arms and lying in bed all day, saying and doing nothing.

Mrs T. Bolus,
Spittle

INDECISIVE about committing suicide? Then hang yourself with a bungee rope.

Peter Carl Fenwick,
Co. Durham

IF you have a squeaking door, leave the house and walk fifty yards down the street. From this distance it is unlikely you will be able to hear it.

Mr S. F. Chicken,
Walter Wilsons

CHARITIES trying to raise money for a new hospice. Forget it and announce plans to build an opera house instead. That way the lottery will pay for it. Once it's finished, simply rip out the seats and replace them with beds for the terminally ill.

S.L. House,
Norwich

SALES reps. Place an 'honesty box' on the dashboard of your car. Every time you speed, fine yourself £5. At the end of each year the money you raise can then be used to buy a large fully-equipped hospital to treat all the people who've been killed or injured as a result of your reckless driving.

B.B.,
Newmarket

DON'T waste money on gift vouchers this Christmas. Try giving bank notes. These are available in a variety of sizes, colours and denominations, and are accepted by most High Street shops.

C. McKeown,
Fleetwood

TRANSFORM your garage into an American style 'drive-in' restaurant by sitting in your car, lowering your window and

demanding that your wife brings you a cup of tea on roller skates.

S. Safeway,
Surbiton

PROMISE to ring people at specific times, and then don't. They'll ring you to see what's wrong, at which point you can have your original planned conversation at their expense.

Dawn Ralphson,
Lancs

REMOVE the small plastic beads from cheap necklaces and slip them into your kids' food. You'll then be able to easily identify their stools at a later date, should the need to do so arise.

E. Reid,
Ely

AVOID being wheel-clamped by jacking your car up, removing the wheels and locking them safely in the boot till you return.

Angus Can, Oxfordshire

CREATE 'lightning' in your fish tank by lowering a fork into the water then briefly connecting it to the electricity supply.

S. Thomson,
Wemyss Bay

RACE track owners. 'Sleeping policemen' and other traffic calming measures would help reduce the number of serious accidents during Grand Prix races.

Mrs S.F. Brains,
Winchester

NOLAN SISTERS

UNDERWATER *camera-men. Don't throw away those old discarded supermarket trolleys. Tied together with string two of them make a handy anti shark cage.*
Hapag Lloyd, Runcorn

BUY *onions instead of apples. They are always much cheaper.*
Mrs A. Osborne, London

WHEN *embarking on a new relationship always lend your partner twenty quid. That way, when you inevitably get chucked, at least you get your money back thus cheering up an otherwise miserable day.*
A. Rolph, Chelmsford

LADIES. *A toilet freshener in your handbag helps keep it smelling fresh.*
Jackie P., Bolton

DISTURBED *American teenagers. Develop a more balanced perspective on life by listening to Ossie Osbourne's Suicide Solution immediately followed by Queen's Don't Try Suicide.*
Boogie, Rhonda

PLASTIC *tops from Smartie tubes make ideal frisbees for a pet gerbil or hamster.*
Eric Waspbottom, Nottingham

PENSIONERS. *Save on heating bills this winter by recalling the moment, at the 1992 pre-election Labour Party Rally, when Neil Kinnock said: "Comrades. Alright! Alright! Well alright!" The thought of it will make you glow from head to foot with embarrassment.*
D. T., Cardiff

BY *simply fixing a mirror to the ceiling it is possible to examine your feet without looking down.*
L. C. Anderson, Paris

WHEN *out driving always turn left. Then, should you become lost, you can find your way home by reversing the procedure and always turning right.*
Mr. B.M.W. Five-Series, Aldershot

PINEAPPLE *rings make attractive tree decorations, and slot easily onto the branches of your tree. Leave the remaining juice in a glass on the mantlepiece - an ideal treat for Santa!*
Mrs I. Jones, Hebden Bridge

MAKE *the postman think you have a severe dental abscess by opening the door with a hard-boiled egg secreted in your cheek.*
Patrick Thistle, Partick Thistle

WHEN *packing expensive objects in a box, popcorn makes an ideal replacement for expensive polystyrene chips.*
Mr Edwards, Leighton Buzzard

NO TIME *for a bath? Wrap yourself in masking tape and remove the dirt by simply peeling it off.*
Dennis Phipps, Blackburn

FILL *a flat fish with hot butter last thing at night and it makes an ideal hot water bottle. Wake up in the morning and 'voila!' A ready-cooked kipper for breakfast in bed.*
Barry Clarver, Exeter

THE LID *from a sardine tin, with the key removed, makes an ideal quiff for a small robot.*
I. Ink, Bootle

IMPRESS *girls this summer by driving up and down the seafront with an ironing board strapped to the roof of your car, and Beach Boys music playing loudly on the stereo.*
B. Meredith, Swansea

A COCKTAIL *stick, marble and a key ring make the perfect javelin, shot putt and hammer for your rodent decathlon.*
A. E. Greenall, Liverpool 12

LADIES. *When commuting to work, try leaving the house five minutes earlier than usual in order that male commuters may be spared the ridiculous spectacle of you trying to 'run' for a train.*
Eric Hoggers, Hayes Middlesex

ASK *your barber to save your hair clippings. In later life these can be made into a wig, and will match your remaining hair perfectly.*
Yasmin Fletcher, Priestley

FELLAS. *Next time you're contemplating masturbation in your bedroom, make sure your bedside lamp is between you and the curtains, to avoid giving neighbours and passers-by an entertaining 'shadow play'.*
J. Holden, Swindon

17

We're all going on a...

SUMMER HOLIDAY

PRETEND you are enjoying a sunny beach holiday by putting sandpaper insoles in your slippers and walking around the house in your underpants, with all the lights turned on.

David Inch, Chester-le-Street

HOLIDAYMAKERS. Avoid the need to pack bulky shampoo bottles which can leak in your suitcase, by arranging for the whole family to have 'skinhead' haircuts a day or two before departure.

Roger Plynth, Polegate

MAKE polystyrene lifebelts for your plant pots and float your house plants in the bath when you go on holiday.

D. Price, Bradford

FOR those who haven't got enough money for two weeks' holiday, go for one week and don't go to bed.

Christopher 'Monty' Heading, Aged 8, Nottingham

OFFICE workers. Top up that fading holiday tan during quiet moments by laying on the photocopier and pressing the 'Copy' button.

Mark Anderson, Hampstead

PRETEND you're a German on holiday by being rude to your neighbours, over-eating at breakfast time, and barging into the queue at the Post Office.

T. Pearson, Hull

RE-KINDLE memories of your summer holiday in sunny Greece by turning off your water supply, removing all toilet roll from your bathroom, placing a dirty bucket next to your toilet and forcing some Plasticine up behind your index finger nail.

Richard B., Thurrock

WHILST on holiday, always wear a paper hat with the date and your holiday destination written clearly on the front. In years to come this will enable you to identify holiday snaps with ease.

Ken Road, Luton

WHEN holidaying abroad, include a toilet brush and standard lamp in your luggage. Hotels rarely provide toilet brushes, and the lamp will come in handy for reading.

Mrs. D. Patterson, Shrewsbury

ASTHMATICS. Avoid going on holiday to places where the scenery is described as breathtaking.

J. Cloth, Bedside Manor

HOLIDAYMAKERS. When catching a ferry or Eurotunnel Shuttle train, jack your car's wheels up off the ground, put your car in gear and continue to 'drive' at exactly the same speed the boat or train is travelling. This will ensure your mileometer shows the true distance your car has travelled during your entire journey.

A. Nugget, Northumberland

GIRLS. Too old to go on an 18-to-30 holiday? Simply get pissed, lie in a sand pit in your garden and shag every bloke who looks at you over the fence.

S. Filler, Fulchester

HOLIDAY makers. Prevent postmen from reading your post cards by sending them all in a sealed envelope to one trusted friend, together with a note asking your friend to deliver them all by hand.

Lorraine Quiche, Banbury

SMOKERS. Enjoy seemingly longer holidays by stopping smoking on your first day off, making every day thereafter appear to be 72 hours long.

Steve Irving, Burbage

SWAP your wife's factor-35 sunblock for Brylcreem on the first day of your foreign holiday. Then when she's confined to the hotel bed with sunstroke, nip out and shag loads of birds from Manchester.

P. Jacobs, Walthamstow

BANGKOK holiday makers. Avoid confusion and potential embarrassment by never banging a woman with a hairier arse than yourself.

Mark Bruce, e-mail

PLANNING holidays is half the fun. So why not stay at home this year and plan two? Just as much fun, and it costs absolutely nothing.

R. Rolaston, Redhill

POST Offices. Put up a notice saying 'Travel Money Available Instantly Here', let people queue up for ten minutes and then advise them that they need to give 3-days' notice to order Euros for the holiday they are going on the next day.

Loz, e-mail

STOP German holiday makers hogging all the deckchairs this summer by getting them to sign an agreement promising not to. Then return to your hotel room and wave it in the air, saying "I have in my hand a piece of paper".

Phil Bert, Leicester

REMOVE your trousers and tie them around your neck before you get into your car. You will then be able to remove your handkerchief, keys or wallet from your trouser pocket with ease, even after you have fastened your seat belt.

J. Varley, London N 18

CARDBOARD hats worn by McDonald's staff make ideal canoes for guinea pigs. And the plastic tea stirrers are perfect oars.

A.E. Greenall, Liverpool 12

AVOID endless arguments with your wife about leaving the toilet seat down by simply pissing in the sink.

A. Toplight, Neville Hill

SAVE electricity by turning off all the lights in your house and walking around wearing a miner's hat.

D. Purvis, Bolton

CAN'T afford contact lenses? Simply cut out small circles of cling film using a paper punch and then press them onto your eyes.

D. Stokes, Middlesex

INCREASE the weight of your husband's trousers by attaching onions to the belt loops.

Uncle Len, Ruddington

A BLACK binliner draped over a TV aerial makes a cheap yet effective umbrella, particularly handy in the wet and blustery spring months.

D. Topper, Woking

ALWAYS buy checked shirts for your husband. Any food stains can then be accurately located using grid references.

Kevin Gildea, Ilford, Essex

ALWAYS carry a tin of white paint and a paint brush in the boot of your car. If your chosen car park is full, simply paint an additional parking space for yourself.

Margaret B. Dickinson, Burnley

HITCHCOCK fans. Glue breadcrumbs to a climbing frame in your garden, then sit on a bench with your back to it. Once the frame is covered in birds, try making a run for the house.

P Todrie, Aberdeen

LADIES. Knock 'em dead at Ascot this year by going into your garage or garden shed, getting the biggest thing you can find and wearing it on your head.

M. Samson, Didburyshire

The Top Tip Detector Van

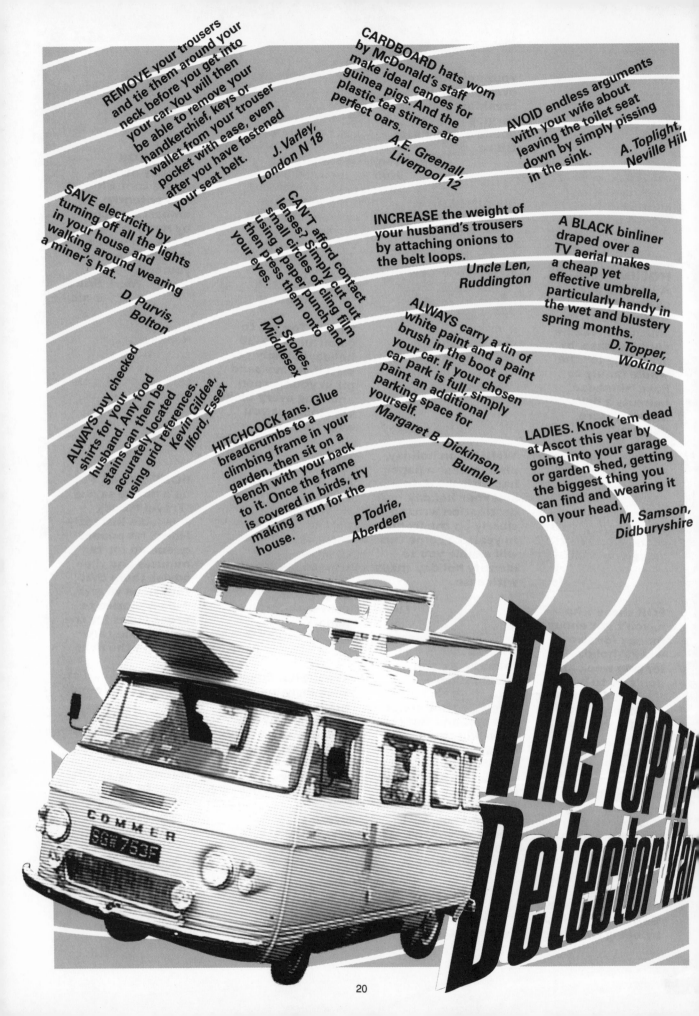

MUMS. A strip of banana peel tacked to the bottom of your children's shoes allows them to be towed effortlessly around supermarkets.

*J. Tait,
Thropton*

AVOID dropped oven gloves from landing on the dirty floor by attaching them to the ceiling with a short length of elastic. As soon as you remove them from your hands the gloves will fly back to the ceiling.

*Mrs B. Harper,
Stoke*

IF you have guests staying overnight, always shave their pillows beforehand. I always do this and have yet to receive a single complaint about feathers protruding.

*Mrs Doris Price,
Berkshire*

SINGLE people. Pretend you're having sex by parking your car in a secluded country lane and steam up your windows using a 'travel kettle' plugged into the cigarette lighter.

*Alastair Green,
e-mail*

A SIMPLE drinking straw, cut into small lengths will make sufficient batons for up to six rodent display teams. Alternatively, one straw makes a first class 'pole' for rodent pole vaulters.

*T. Silver,
Newbury*

IMPRESS visitors by sitting on their lap, flicking through an animal book, and making the appropriate animal noise for each picture.

*Jarnes Taylor,
Sussex*

P.S. This works best if you are under two years old.

CYCLISTS. Why not try stopping at red lights like everyone else, instead of riding up onto the pavement to avoid them. Stupid bastards.

*M. Burridge,
Newcastle*

GIRLS. Don't worry about buying a new dress for that important first date. All he's interested in is seeing you starkers.

I. Cadman, Rotherham

A GOOD book with all the pages covered in cellophane makes for ideal reading in the shower.

*S. Adam,
London*

KEEP the seat next to you on the train vacant by smiling and nodding at people as they walk up the aisle.

*Mrs Deirdre Partridge,
Rugby*

CON passing aeroplane passengers into thinking your house has an outdoor swimming pool by painting a large blue rectangle on your lawn.

*Mr Paul,
Crawley*

ADD an element of danger to your gerbil's boring life by hiding a bowl of Ready Brek under its sawdust with a small sign nearby saying 'Danger - quicksand'.

*Hapag Lloyd,
Runcorn*

POTATOES make interesting if not entirely functional replacements for light bulbs.

*Mrs B. Durks,
Essex*

FELLAS. Make your bird's tits look bigger by viewing them through a magnifying glass.

*G. Knox,
Walsall*

LEARNER skateboarders. Carry an old paint roller in each hand. These can be used as 'stabilisers' whenever you lose your balance.

*Desmond Umbridge,
Bolton*

UNEMPLOYED? Annoy your neighbour by sprinkling nettle and other weed seeds into his flower beds while he's at work.

*Stef Miller,
Sheffield*

MAKE yourself drive more carefully in built-up areas by cutting out pictures of children playing football and glueing them to the sides of your windscreen.

Mr C. Savoury, Yeovil

DRIVERS. Spot traffic build-ups from miles away by mounting a telescope on your dashboard, thus giving you time to take an alternative route.

David Green, Swinton

MOTORISTS. When going through a speed camera, quickly flash your lights twice, and watch the driver in front hit his brakes when he thinks he's been caught.

Kathy, Crewe

DRIVERS. If a car breaks down or stalls in front of you, beep your horn and wave your arms frantically. This should help the car start and send them on their way.

Paul, South Africa

DRIVERS. Save money by putting much larger wheels on the back of your car. That way you will always be going downhill, thereby saving on fuel.

Daren Percy, Leigh

DRIVERS. Avoid being nicked by the new 'average speed' blue cameras by driving at 90mph for two minutes between them, then stopping for a spliff.

Ray Wilson, e-mail

MOTORISTS. Deflate all your tyres before putting 20p in the forecourt air-line machine. That way you'll get your money's worth.

Oliver Hardy, e-mail

4X4 DRIVERS. Use your bullbars as a handy mobile railing on which you can tie flowers in memory of the people you run down.

M. Trouserman, Birmingham

MAKE your car much easier to find in a large car park by letting down all the tyres. On your return simply look for the lowest car.

Bill Norman, Cardiff

LORRY drivers. Look down the wrong end of a pair of binoculars when driving on the motorway. This will enable you to drive even closer to the back of my fucking car.

L. Ripper, Westward Ho!

AVOID parking tickets by leaving your windscreen wipers turned on to 'fast wipe' whenever you leave your car parked illegally.

S. Tyler, Norwich

IF DRIVING your car quickly over speed bumps causes your exhaust to come loose, try reversing over them. It should tighten everything up.

Martin, Bradford

ELDERLY drivers. Pressing the pedal on your right will make your car go a little faster. Forget all that rubbish about suffocating at speeds above 15mph, it was all a myth.

Oliver Hardy, e-mail

MOTORISTS. Pressing your fog lights switch a second time after the fog has cleared will actually turn the fog lights off.

J.C., Luton

DRIVERS. Drop gravel into your fuel tank so you can fill your car up for less at the petrol station.

Frank Randle, Clitheroe

MOTORISTS. Avoid costly MOTs by simply booking an MOT test on every day of the year. Then if the police stop you, you can say you were on your way to get an MOT.

J. Barnes, e-mail

MOTORISTS. Avoid getting prosecuted for using your phone whilst driving. Simply pop your mobile inside a large shell and the police will think you are listening to the sea.

A. Corten, Caerleon

FOOL neighbours into thinking your car is automatic by selecting reverse momentarily before driving off.

M. Johnson, Leigh-on-Sea

HOMEOWNERS. Avoid losing your keys during the day by simply leaving them in the door as you leave the house in the morning.

**B. Sparks,
Luton**

HOMEOWNERS. Avoid coming home to find your video gone, your widescreen TV smashed because it was too heavy to carry and a big steaming turd in the middle of the carpet by not leaving your keys in the door in the morning.

**B. Sparks,
Luton**

WHEN tickling a friend or relative, try saying "tickie-tickie! Tickie-tickie!" as this guarantees around 37% more laughter than standard silent tickling.

**Bridie Boo,
e-mail**

RATS. Improve your image by attaching a small brush to your arse and pretending to be a squirrel.

**Colin Saunders,
e-mail**

FELLAS. Pretend that you are TV's Anthony McPartlin out of Ant and Dec, by looking at yourself in the back of a spoon.

**Mark Hudson,
e-mail**

BREAST MEN. When shopping in the supermarket, miss out the first aisle so that you are going against the flow. Arse men should follow the usual route.

**Spike,
e-mail**

LADIES. Take all the tips from *Chat* magazine and send them to *Take A Break*. It's a nice little earner, and the mindless zombie publishers will neither know nor care.

**Ben,
Swansea**

EMO kids. Get revenge on everyone that 'doesn't care' by cutting yourself in unseen places. That'll show 'em.

**DJ Ants,
e-mail**

TEENAGERS. Make sure your dad doesn't find out you've been watching his porn films by not whistling the theme tune to *Emmanuelle* at the dinner table.

**Richard Bowen,
e-mail**

SOLVE 'Spot the Difference' puzzles by relaxing your eyes until you see four pictures. Then move the pictures backwards or forwards until the two middle ones overlap and then mark off the 10 locations where something appears not to be quite right.

**Andrew Tait,
Newcastle**

SAVE money on tap shoes by simply pushing drawing pins into the toes and heels of your feet.

**Bruno Tonioli,
e-mail**

GAMBLERS. For a new gambling opportunity, try sending a £50 to yourself by Royal Mail.

**Chris,
London**

LETTERBOCKS fans. Save yourself a few quid every deci-month by picking up a free copy of *Metro* every day. Most of the letters in *Viz* get reprinted in there eventually.

**F. Muir,
London**

GREEN pet owners. A cigarette filter shoved up your cat's arse makes an ideal 'catalytic converter' to remove the environmentally-harmful methane from its farts.
Stu Mandry,
e-mail

PREVENT the inconvenience of waiting for energy-saving fluorescent lightbulbs to brighten up by simply leaving them switched on all the time.
Matt Salisbury,
e-mail

SAVE energy by placing solar-powered calculators under a hat when not in use.
Don Croy,
Surrey

UTILITY companies. Encourage customers to go to 'paperless billing' and online account management to help the environment. It has the added benefit of rendering them helpless when you overcharge them as they have no bills to check through and your computer can mysteriously 'freeze' their on-line account'. It makes it almost impossible for them to prove you are a bunch of robbing bastards.
Jay, e-mail

ENVIRON-MENTALLY friendly masturbators. Use one of the socks you have worn that day as your evening wank sock. The sock would have required washing anyway, thus reducing your carbon footprint.
Branwell Govier,
e-mail

MEN. Save energy drying recently washed pots and pans by blasting each of them for 30 seconds in the microwave.
Peter Smith,
e-mail

GREEN TIPS

with Sting out of The Police.

FOOL neighbours into thinking your car has an expensive alarm fitted by sleeping in it every night, turning your hazard lights on and constantly sounding the horn at regular intervals.

M. Planck,
Stafford

AVOID embarrassing yourself when drunk by taking large quantities of booze to a shed at the bottom of your garden and drinking it all in there.

B and D,
Bristol

PIG farmers. Paint toilet roll tubes black, then fill them with snow. Hey presto! Liquorice Allsorts for pigs, with no sugar to harm their teeth.

K. Wharton,
Stamford

SAVE electricity by turning off all the lights in your house and walking around wearing a miner's hat.

D. Purvis,
Bolton

LUMPS of cheese make perfect 'Lego'-style building bricks for kids. They're cheap and they're fun, and there's no trips to casualty every time they happen to swallow a piece. And they give a whole new meaning to the the idea of 'playing with your food'.

S. Filler,
Fulchester

WHEN reading a book try tearing out the pages as you read them. This saves the expense of buying a bookmark, and the pages can later be Tippexed over and used for shopping lists.

Mrs P. Hamilton,
Arbroath

RECREATE the fun of a visit to a public swimming pool in your own home by filling the bath with cold water, adding two bottles of bleach, then urinating into it, before jumping in.

Mrs S. Poole,
Bath

PLACE a small table behind your front door in order to avoid bending down to pick up the post.

N. Blackett-Ord,
Ashton-under-Lyne

FELLAS. When out shopping, be careful not to get binliners and panty-liners confused. I have it on good authority that neither is much good as a substitute for the other.

Tony Silver,
Newbury

AVOID paying tax by going to work in a politically-unstable Middle East country inhabited by religious fanatics. Ignore British Government advice to leave when a war looks imminent, then moan a few

weeks later when bombs start going off and there aren't any planes home.

S. Goblin,
Middlesex

TOASTERS make ideal 'daredevil' cannons for flat fish such as flounder, sole or turbot. But fish should be careful to perform this trick on dry land only, as water is an excellent conductor of electricity.

Sean Phillips,
Dundee

OLD biddies. Easter will neither be 'very late' nor 'very early' this year. So that's one less interminable conversation you can have with each other.

Dave Stuttard,
Warrington

SAVE the call charge next time you dial a wrong number by replacing your receiver before the phone is answered.

Mike Way, Rodingham

MASHED potato looks a bit like snow, and is harmless for children.

H. Civic,
Southampton

TRAMPS. Stand with a paper cup next to the nearest bottle bank. Ask visitors to pour any remaining drops from their bottles into your cup. Within a few minutes you will have a free cup full of alcoholic punch.

Mr T. Tart,
Sainsburys

A SWISH curtain rail, a pyjama cord and a hat pin provide a cheap but effective bow and arrow for Robin Hood games in the park. Alternatively, in these safety conscious times, why not substitute a sink plunger for the hat pin?

Mrs D. Treliss, Colwyn Bay

HALF a table tennis ball with an elastic band attached makes an ideal 'safety helmet' for your pet hamster, and significantly reduces the risk of head injury should he fall whilst using his exercise wheel.

Mr C. Cream, Bisley

CARRY a different vegetable in your pocket each weekday to remind you what day it is. For example: Sunday- a sprout, Monday- a marrow, Tuesday- a turnip, Wednesday ... etc.

I. Tobacco, Bradford

MANCHESTER United fans. Avoid an asymmetrical muscular bulge on your right arm by masturbating alternately with your left hand.

Gregory Clarke, London NW4

DON'T put washing-up liquid in the garage or loft. Keep it handy in the kitchen. I put mine in the cupboard under the sink.

L. Bowman, Tulsa

WELL-TO-DO middle and upper class people. Avoid feelings of guilt due to your privileged lifestyle by going to church regularly and prescribing to a doctrine based upon one or other interpretation of certain parts of the Bible. Simply re-interpret - or completely ignore - any parts of the Bible which are incompatible with your own lifestyle of greed and affluence.

Mr S. Ford-Bridges, London SW1

IF you feel someone is taking an unreasonable length of time to answer the phone, punish them by putting the receiver down the second they eventually answer.

Ben Collins, Sunderland

ONE way of keeping hot cooked sausages safe from children is by putting them on a work surface and fixing them down with brightly coloured sticky tape.

Mrs E. Bosomworth, London

VIDEO your goldfish swimming in its bowl, then place your TV set next to the bowl, and play back the tape. Hey presto! Instant 'company' for your fish. Duplicate the tape and use extra televisions to create a 'goldfish party' for special occasions.

Mrs B. Lane, Aston Clinton, Bucks.

SKIN a tomato by simply eating it. Hey presto! The next day you are left with just the skin in the toilet pan.

John Tait, Thropton

HAT wearers. Beat the wind by wearing a fuzzy head-band and stitching a strip of Velcro around the inside of your hat .

Brian C. Smith, Edinburgh

USING string, nails and pulleys it is possible to turn on your hot water tap in the bathroom from the bedroom. By the time you walk to the bathroom the water will have warmed up.

E. Barnpot, Devon

POT HOLERS. Save the emergency services time and money by pot-holing in your own bathroom at night. With the lights off, crawl through a bath full of water, under the sink, then get your head stuck in the toilet. Wait for your wife to wake up and rescue you.

J. Moss, Washington

WHEN shopping for shoes I always write my shoe size on a small piece of paper and tuck it into the top of my sock. This saves me having to remove one of my shoes every time I go into a shop.

Mrs F. Tilbrook, Dunstable

ENLARGE your living space by removing that bulky light shade and gluing sea shells directly onto the bulb.

Doris Pratt, Billingham

OUTDATED 'Mutant Ninja Turtle' figures, painted red or blue, make ideal 'Power Rangers' or 'Pokemons'.

A.G., Liverpool

With Chris Tarrant & Sally James

MAKE your neighbours think you're a doctor by leaving the house in the middle of the night carrying a small leather bag, then returning home half an hour later. Repeat this action up to six times every night.
P.C., Leicester

ASK your butcher to thinly slice those old Wellington boots, and he y presto! An endless supply of wind-screen wiper blades.
D.N., Farnborough

OPEN air swimming pools get little use in winter. So why not fill them with soil and grow flowers in them until the summer comes round again.
Glen Dale, Northumberland

SAVE money by not buying a Big Country single. Simply listen to the theme from BBC TV's Z Cars instead. P. Goss, Basildon

KEEP a few ten pence pieces in your pyjama pocket in case you are abducted by aliens during the night and need to phone home.
H. Lord, Redcar

STAR Trek security officers. If you have never appeared in the programme before and sud-denly Captain Kirk asks you to join a landing party, make an excuse. Under no circumstances should you beam down to the planet surface, as you will invariably be killed.
Mr L Hall, Northumberland

WHY waste money on expensive answering machines? When you leave the house simply plug your phone into the video recorder. Not only will it record the caller's voice, but you'll also get a TV picture of them speaking. Probably.
T. J. Jones, Valenton

SAVE a fortune on expensive hotel breakfasts by keeping a few rashers of streaky bacon, or a couple of kippers in your overnight bag. Pop them into the trouser press provided before you go to bed, and wake up to the aroma of fresh-ly grilled bacon, or smoked kippers.
Derrick Carleton, Penrith

OLD folks. Avoid confusion between your new 'microwave' oven and televi-sion set by cutting out a large letter 'M' in brightly coloured paper, and sticking it to the door of the oven.
Mrs G. Jones, Leicester

WEAR trousers back to front. That way you'll never get the little fella' caught in your zip.
G. Adams, Croydon

neopost
FLIGHT
3.00PM.!!

BEAT bicycle theft by tow-ing a horse box behind your bike. When you stop, simply padlock the cycle securely inside the horse box.
Don Brayford, Suffolk

lose weight quickly by eating raw pork or rancid tuna. I found that the subsequent food poisoning/diarrhoea enabled me to lose 12 pounds in only two days.   K. dellassus. newcastle

TO avoid losing keys every time you put them down ring a friend and tell him where you put them. Later, if you can't find them, simply ring your friend and ask him where they are.
Peter Evans, Br

GAUGE local night-time wind conditions by installing an ultra sensitive alarm in your soft-top sports car. The most moderate of gusts will activate the alarm and keep both yourself and your neighbours fully informed as to local wind conditions.

M. Retard, Cambridge

I ENJOY drinking ..... but can't afford the expense. So instead of drinking beer I simply gargle it then spit it back into my glass. That way, I can make one pint last me all evening.

Dave Parker, Avon

I HAVE always found it helpful to unfasten the zip at the front of my trousers before urinating.

R. Head, Durham

WHEN photographing windmills, attach a white handkerchief to the end of one of the sails. When your picture is developed this will prove invaluable in indicating both wind direction and sail rotation.

R Well, Holland

STOP to pick up the bodies of any small animals (rabbits, mice, weasels, etc) which you run over on the road, and keep them in the boot of your car. Once the boot is full you should have enough to make a fur coat – an ideal surprise gift for your wife.

P Parker, Preston

PRETEND you have dry rot by filling your sub floor void with candy floss.

S. Cooper, Tring

EAT whilst watching TV without having to take your eyes off the screen for a second. Simply cover your plate with tin foil and wire it up to your fork with a battery and bell. If the fork touches an area of plate with no food on it, the bell will sound and you can simply try again.

Dave Simpson, Tring

...TCH a monkey by ...ling a hole in a hollow ...e just wide enough for ...monkey's hand to pass ...rough, then put nuts ...de the hole. The mon-...de the tree to reach ...will stick his hand ...m, but with the nuts ...his grasp his hand will ...too wide to remove ...in the hole. The ...mal will not have the ...elligence to drop the ...s in order to effect ...escape

...till, Birmingham

...-sized
...rs bars
...e ideal
...al-sized
...rs bars
...dwarfs,

T. Dell...
Southampton

EAT soup whilst watching TV by wiring up a simple lighting circuit with two terminals in your bowl so that when both are exposed to air and the bowl is empty the circuit breaks and a light above the TV goes out. Wear rubber gloves for extra safety whilst eating.

Dave Simpson, Tring

DON'T INVITE DRUG ADDICTS ROUND FOR A MEAL ON BOXING DAY. THEY MAY FIND THE OFFER OF COLD TURKEY EMBARRASSING OR OFFENSIVE.

STEVEN HOWLETT
LONDON

VARNISH digestive biscuits to make attractive, if slightly brittle, drinks coasters.

B. Thompson, Houston

FILL the bath with water, then add 14 kilos of salt. Hey presto! Your own miniature 'Dead Sea'.

Steven James, Stoke on Trent

PLANNING a kids' party? Remember to make your cactus plants safe for the children by removing all the spines with a pair of tweezers.

Gillian Tasker, Derbyshire

MUMS. Save money when buying skimmed milk by buying full fat milk instead, then simply diluting it at home with water.

Mr C. Day, Milton Keynes

PENSIONERS. Avoid the embarrassment of having your swollen, badly-beaten face shown on the front cover of newspapers by keeping a reasonable amount of cash in your home. Only if your attacker nets a paltry amount will the tabloids show any interest.

A. Anderson, Hereford

MAKE people think you have an expensive car phone by calling them, asking them to repeat everything they say, then hanging up half-way through their reply.

Mr I. Baxter, Exemouth

TWO spaghetti hoops make an ideal pair of reading glasses for gingerbread men.

Mrs L. H., Longhorsely

A DROP of cooking oil placed outside their hole will help get rid of mice. When they next appear, they will slip over onto their backs, making capture much easier.

Lynne Bordessa, Allerton

VICARS. Drum up more business this winter by dressing as Santa Claus and starting your Christmas services in early October.

D. Robinson, Cramlington

SATELLITE TV enthusiasts. Save the expense of a motorised dish system by installing a fixed dish to the roof of your car. Then simply drive round in small circles until you locate the satellite of your choice.

John Kean, Satcom Europe Ltd.

LADIES. When invited out to dinner in a fashionable restaurant always bring a fire blanket with you in your bag. Nowadays it is the foolhardy fashion for waiters to set fire to the pudding, and there is always a risk that the blaze could get out of control.

Miss B. Baxter, Potters Bar

WHEN dining in restaurants don't start eating until every course has been brought to the table. With your whole order laid out in front of you it is much easier to check the bill when it arrives.

F. Consul, Leeds

REMOVE the laces from any odd boots and shoes which you find washed up on the beach. Pop them inside a sock next time you wash any clothes, then dry them with an iron and keep them in an old yoghurt carton for use as spares.

A. Houndog, Cumbria

DON'T waste money on these expensive 'binoculars'. Simply stand closer to the object you wish to see.

S. Goldhanger, Fulchester

Michael Jackson

30

ON TRAINS, the plastic triangular packs in which sandwiches are sold make ideal elbow protectors. Wear them on your sleeves to prevent your elbows getting wet when your coffee gets spilled all over the table.

C. A. Mints, Fulham

GUN clubs. Ban quiet, shy men who tend to 'keep themselves to themselves'. Invariably these are the people who go berserk and carry out random, pointless shootings of innocent passers by.

T. Starlet, Arbroath

TINNED sweetcorn fans. Save yourself the bother of wiping your arse by emptying the tin straight into the toilet.

T. O., Sussex

TRAIL a six foot length of toilet tissue along your bathroom floor, over the rim of your lavatory bowl and into the water. Flush the toilet and then watch as the tissue is 'eaten' by the bowl, like someone sucking in spaghetti.

A. Tait, Newcastle

WHEN on those forest walks, scatter pebbles along the way in order to find your way back. The birds can't eat them, and you won't end up at some stupid witch's toffee house in the middle of nowhere.

H & G, Bavaria

WHEN having grandmothers or other elderly relatives cremated, always ask the undertaker for their false teeth. These make excellent pastry cutters, and the decorative crust of a pork pie can evoke many happy memories of your loved one.

A. Richardson, Carlisle

AVOID peak hour congestion between Stirling and Glasgow at the A80 Auchinkilns roundabout by taking the A8011 through Cumbernauld and rejoining the A80 beyond this bottleneck.

G. Keddie, Glasgow

MODERNISE old-fashioned 'drainpipe' trousers by making a slit in each leg and sewing in triangles of cloth removed from a length of bunting. Hey presto! Fashionable flares.

J. Black, Fulchester

FOR MANY years I've kepy my legs warm in winter by wearing ladies' tights beneath my trousers. I've never found it embarrassing, as they make perfectly good - and economical - leg warmers. As a pensioner, saving money and staying warm are my priorities. In summer I switch to wearing cooler and more hygienic stockings and suspenders.

Mr A. Cream, Rotherham

KEEP old Lottery tickets until Christmas. Cut into strips they make 'instant' paper chains for decorating your room with, and a useful reminder of how much money you've blown throughout the year.

Steven Wood, Nottingham

REDUCE wear and tear on your work clothes by 20% by simply staying in bed on Mondays and not going to work.

T. Sponge, Dunbar

IMPRESS members of the opposite sex by acquiring a comprehensive knowledge of a subject which interests them and then steering the conversation towards this topic.

Paul Armstrong, Manchester

A FEW drops of car engine oil mixed with treacle will help it flow more easily from the tin. I would imagine.

Dave Moore, Nottingham

MRS TOM Jones. Prevent your husband from bursting on a hot day by pricking him several times with a fork.

E. Hoover, Leeds

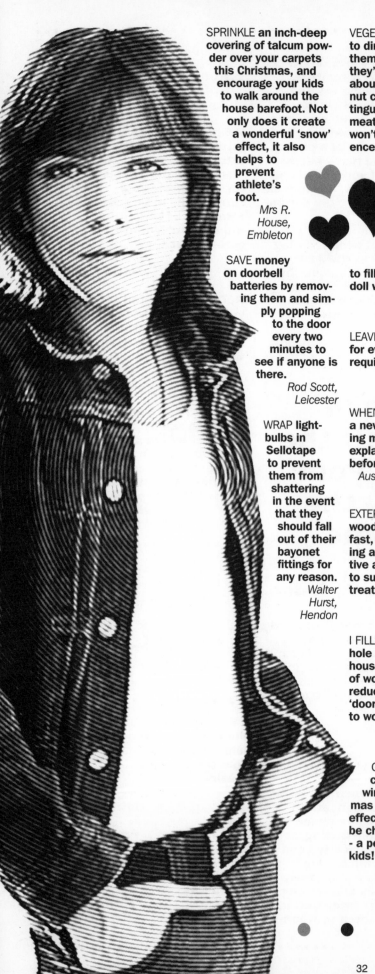

SPRINKLE an inch-deep covering of talcum powder over your carpets this Christmas, and encourage your kids to walk around the house barefoot. Not only does it create a wonderful 'snow' effect, it also helps to prevent athlete's foot.

Mrs R. House, Embleton

SAVE money on doorbell batteries by removing them and simply popping to the door every two minutes to see if anyone is there.

Rod Scott, Leicester

WRAP lightbulbs in Sellotape to prevent them from shattering in the event that they should fall out of their bayonet fittings for any reason.

Walter Hurst, Hendon

VEGETARIANS coming to dinner? Simply give them real meat. As they're always going on about how TVP soya and nut cutlets are "indistinguishable from real meat nowadays", they won't notice the difference.

S. Simpson, Edgeware

FELLAS. A fun way to keep warm on cold winter nights is to fill your inflatable sex doll with hot water.

Pete Turner, Garston

LEAVE one curtain open for every pint of milk you require in the morning.

Austin Cambridge, Southwick

WHENEVER you introduce a new system for ordering milk, make sure you explain it to the milkman beforehand.

Austin Cambridge, Southwick

EXTERIOR wood stain is a fast, long-lasting and attractive alternative to sun-bed treatments.

Mr T. Eebly, Wanstead

I FILLED the rectangular hole at the front of my house with a flat piece of wood. As well as reducing heat loss, my 'door' is also a deterrent to would-be burglars.

A. Tenanty, Sheffield

GLUE desiccated coconut to your windows this Christmas for a perfect 'snow' effect. Afterwards it can be chiseled off and fried - a perfect treat for the kids!

Mrs I. Jones, Hebden Bridge

SMOKERS. Save £££s every year on matches and cigarette lighters by simply lighting your cigarette with the butt of your previous one.

T. O'Meara, Brighton

TEENAGERS. Fed up with posters falling off the wall? Simply file them in a filing cabinet under 'P' and you'll know exactly where to find them if you want a quick look.

John Kean, Sheffield

SAVE on expensive washing powder by stealing your neighbours' clean washing from their lines.

E. K. Wright, Ashington

IMPRESS friends by making a list of all the objects in your front room and then inviting them over to play 'I Spy'. Watch their faces as you keep winning!

J. Cowell, Milton Keynes

MAKE sure your neighbour hasn't wired his house up to your electricity supply by asking him to turn on every electric appliance in his house, then sit and watch your meter to see whether it is moving any faster.

F.D., Cardiff

CAR tyres painted white and wrapped in green tarpaulin sheets make ideal packets of Polos for short-sighted giants.

E. F. Gee, Aitchaye

FILL a shoebox with snow, then shit on it. Hey presto! Expensive Belgian chocolates.

Phil Thunderchunk, Ipswich

CASSIDY

DAVID

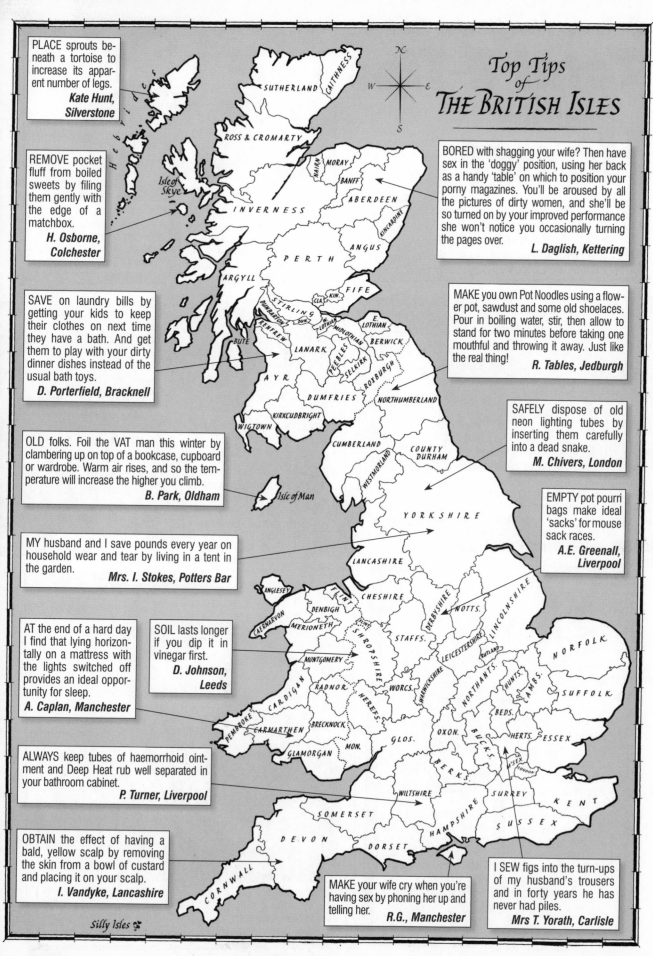

Top Tips of THE BRITISH ISLES

PLACE sprouts beneath a tortoise to increase its apparent number of legs.
Kate Hunt, Silverstone

REMOVE pocket fluff from boiled sweets by filing them gently with the edge of a matchbox.
H. Osborne, Colchester

SAVE on laundry bills by getting your kids to keep their clothes on next time they have a bath. And get them to play with your dirty dinner dishes instead of the usual bath toys.
D. Porterfield, Bracknell

OLD folks. Foil the VAT man this winter by clambering up on top of a bookcase, cupboard or wardrobe. Warm air rises, and so the temperature will increase the higher you climb.
B. Park, Oldham

MY husband and I save pounds every year on household wear and tear by living in a tent in the garden.
Mrs. I. Stokes, Potters Bar

AT the end of a hard day I find that lying horizontally on a mattress with the lights switched off provides an ideal opportunity for sleep.
A. Caplan, Manchester

SOIL lasts longer if you dip it in vinegar first.
D. Johnson, Leeds

ALWAYS keep tubes of haemorrhoid ointment and Deep Heat rub well separated in your bathroom cabinet.
P. Turner, Liverpool

OBTAIN the effect of having a bald, yellow scalp by removing the skin from a bowl of custard and placing it on your scalp.
I. Vandyke, Lancashire

MAKE your wife cry when you're having sex by phoning her up and telling her.
R.G., Manchester

BORED with shagging your wife? Then have sex in the 'doggy' position, using her back as a handy 'table' on which to position your porny magazines. You'll be aroused by all the pictures of dirty women, and she'll be so turned on by your improved performance she won't notice you occasionally turning the pages over.
L. Daglish, Kettering

MAKE you own Pot Noodles using a flower pot, sawdust and some old shoelaces. Pour in boiling water, stir, then allow to stand for two minutes before taking one mouthful and throwing it away. Just like the real thing!
R. Tables, Jedburgh

SAFELY dispose of old neon lighting tubes by inserting them carefully into a dead snake.
M. Chivers, London

EMPTY pot pourri bags make ideal 'sacks' for mouse sack races.
A.E. Greenall, Liverpool

I SEW figs into the turn-ups of my husband's trousers and in forty years he has never had piles.
Mrs T. Yorath, Carlisle

Silly Isles

33

Theirs was a love based on Top Tips...
Total E-Tips
of the
Heart

Trish Copperfield had been going out with hunky Barry Borthwick for six weeks. From the outside, they looked like the perfect couple, but they had a dark secret that threatened to tear them apart... for they could only speak to each other in Top Tips...

LAMB for dinner tonight and forgotten the mint sauce? No worries. Toothpaste mixed with a little vinegar and chopped nettle leaves makes an ideal emergency replacement.
J. T., Thropton

CUT your man's hair around a mousse ring mould instead of a pudding bowl if he is balding at the crown.
Mrs C. Sidiros, Greenford

HELP blind people in the Post Office by licking their stamps for them. Or better still, teach their dogs to do so.
Mr Beakey, Byker

STOP bread from drying out by keeping it in a bucket of water.
P. J. Ruddock, London

The strain soon began to tell on Barry...

...he had to say something...

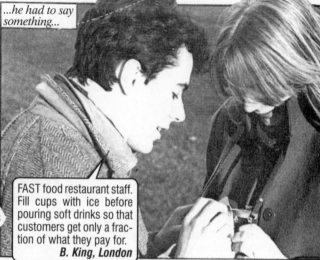

FAST food restaurant staff. Fill cups with ice before pouring soft drinks so that customers get only a fraction of what they pay for.
B. King, London

Suddenly...

GREENGROCERS. Why throw away old, shrivelled, unsold fruit and veg? Simply label it 'Organic Produce' and charge twice the usual price.
P. T., Liverpool L 19

AN IDEAL yet inexpensive Christmas gift for the smoker is a novelty cigarette lighter made from an ordinary house brick with a match tied onto it with a piece of string.
D. Parkinson, Banbury

Trish was in turmoil. She had to have time to think.

MAKE chocolate flavour toothpaste by eating a Mars bar whilst brushing your teeth.
Adam Creen, Newbury

SAVE money on mouthwash by spitting it back into the bottle. Replace the entire bottle once it becomes chewy.
G. T., Shipley

OLD FOLK. Keep your living room warm in winter by plugging in your electric iron and using it as a door stop.
Michael Harby, Bakewell

OVERWEIGHT, unemployed men. Get a well paid job in pantomime this winter by wearing a leotard and a long blonde wig. If you smile enough and flex your arms a bit, you'll be mistaken for a glamorous female 'Gladiator'.
J. Thwaite, Hull

Suddenly...

PLACE your television in the porch and sit outside watching movies through the letter box. Hey presto! An Instant 'widescreen' effect at no extra cost.
D. Scott, Buxton

All of Barry's dreams came true in that one kiss...

But then...

MAKE guests believe your house may be bugged by running your hands under tables and inside lamp shades and turning on the shower every time you want to speak.
C. Rumple, Balham

AMAZE your family by secretly making a pretend candle out of a banana, adding an almond at the top for a flame. Then watch their faces as you eat it!
T. Atack, Pontefract

COVER up circular holes in your kitchen table top by placing a round bread board over the top of them.
Mike Howarth, Manchester

TAKE a Thermos flask to bed instead of a hot water bottle. The water stays hot much longer, and you can use it to make a cup of tea in the morning.
S. T. W., Bristol

HOUSEWIVES. Throw a fish carcass into a bucket of cement, and hey presto! You have an instant fossil.
Tarn Dale, Glasgow

So...

USED lamp bulbs painted green make ideal 'pears' for display in a fruit bowl. They never rot, and will not attract insects.
F. Cooper, Ipswich

NEVER attempt to fasten your shoe laces in a revolving supermarket door.
Mr M. Adeye, Plumstead Infirmary

GENTLEMEN. Never smoke a cigar larger than your penis as this may invite witticisms from former partners.
J. Askey, Bournemouth

POOR people. Can't afford smoked salmon? Simply eat the rubber off an old table tennis bat.
I. Morris, Tiverton

BEFORE attempting to remove stubborn stains from a garment, circle the stain in permanent marker pen. When you remove the garment from your washing machine you can easily find where the stain was and check to make sure it has gone.
E. Williams, Solihull

THE END

STUDENTS. On trains why not dump your rucksack on the seat next to you instead of the luggage rack provided. This will ensure that taxpayers have to stand throughout their journey while you sit back in your subsidised seat, talking loudly.

Eric Hoggers,
Hayes, Middlesex

DON'T throw away that old pianola just because the music rolls are no longer available from record shops. I find that a roll of kitchen paper makes an ideal substitute, although the tune can be somewhat repetitive.

Mrs E. McLane,
Longbenton

FISHERMEN. A dead rabbit makes an ideal growbag for maggots.

Pam Anahat,
Huddersfield

VOLVO drivers. Confuse distant oncoming drivers by removing the bulbs from your sidelights.

P. Delaney,
Greenhills. Dublin

DON'T throw away left-over chips. Pop them in a shoebox inside the freezer. Six months later heat them up in the microwave. Hey presto! Exciting American-style french fries.

Mrs Daisy Pengelly,
Redruth

FARMERS. Minor skin grafts can be performed on pigs by covering any cuts and grazes with thin strips of bacon.

Phil Wasey,
Liverpool

KEEP a tin of red paint handy in your car. If you see an accident you can quickly pour it over yourself and pretend to be involved.

J. Mitchell,
Southampton

AVOID 'red eye' when taking flash photographs by sticking a small piece of black tape over the flash bulb on the front of your camera.

D. Burton,
Felling

SAVE electricity on freezing winter nights by unplugging your fridge and placing the contents on your doorstep.

L. Lipton,
Lanarkshire

GIVE your clothes that 'Elvis Sparkle' by allowing a snail to crawl all over you.

J. Elvis,
Jarrow

A HERD of cattle make a common sense replacement for noisy lawn mowers. Since buying mine I no longer need to mow the lawn, and never have to

worry about the milkman being late.

Mrs R. Dunning,
Leeds

DON'T write your PIN number on the back of your cash card because you won't be able to read it once you've put it in the machine.

William Quibble,
Fyfield

WHY waste a fortune on expensive telephone sex lines? Just dial any number and forget to add the '1' after the first zero. The woman on the BT tape has got a really sexy voice, and the call is free.

Pippa Leg,
Lyndhurst

ENCOURAGE friends to telephone you by offering a free plastic dinosaur for every call you receive.

Hapag Lloyd,
Runcorn

MAKE the postman think you've had a nose bleed by opening the door with tomato ketchup smeared on your top lip.

Patrick Thistle, Partick Thistle

GENTS. Save vital seconds in the morning by urinating in the sink whilst you brush your teeth.

Gary,
Hants.

'NIPPERS' from hermit crabs make ideal clothes pegs for Barbie dolls.

John Tait,
Thropton

Gladys Knight & the Tips

PRETEND your house is a 'Bed & Breakfast' establishment by ordering an extra ten pints of milk each day, and placing a 'Bed & Breakfast' sign in your front window. Unwanted callers can be dissuaded by adding a simple 'No Vacancies' notice.

A. Conway, Dundee

DIVIDE your lawn into a grid using string and wooden pegs. You can then describe your exact position in the garden over the phone to a friend or relative many miles away who would then be able to plot your movements on a piece of graph paper.

R. H. Lorimer, Peebles

AVOID the dangers of cycling on Britain's overcrowded roads by simply making a video of your next car journey and then watching it whilst pedalling away on an exercise bike in front of your television.

Pete T., Liverpool

GET the feel of camping outdoors without the inconvenience by turning off your heating, releasing ants on your bedroom carpet, crapping on the floor, then sleeping on it, wrapped in a plastic bin liner.

Graeme Marsh, Ashford

NEXT time you pop out to the supermarket, glue carpet tiles to the soles of your shoes. They'll make Sainsburys feel like your own living room.
D.P, Bath

SPECTACLE wearers. Stand at your local car wash on Sunday mornings and ask successive drivers if they wouldn't mind hanging your glasses from their radiator grille while they wash their car.
R. M., Southampton

CAREER women. Save time getting ready for work by putting on five pairs of pants on Monday. Then each morning simply whip off the top pair and hey presto! There's a clean pair underneath.
S. Stain, London

LOCAL councils. Instead of wasting money putting speed humps all over the place, simply make anyone convicted of speeding put egg-shaped wheels on their cars.
Paddy O'Faggot, e-mail

THE FOUR TOP TIPS

TOP CRIME TIPS WITH... THE SWEENEY

POLICE. Get prime seats for your local panto this year by stopping one of the stars as they drive home after the show full of drink. They're bound to offer you free tickets.

P. Noble, Torquay

EVERY day make a list of everything you do, and hand it in at your local police station. That way you can be eliminated from their enquiries in the event of a crime.

D. Anon, Monkchester

PREVENT burglars stealing everything in the house by simply moving everything in the house into your bedroom when you go to bed. In the morning, simply move it all back again.

Anthony Smales, Beverley

BURGLARS. When fleeing from the police, run with your right arm sticking out at 90°, wrapped in a baby mattress in case they set one of their dogs on you.

P. Frampton, Chichester

JOYRIDERS. Lie in the freezer all day before going out at night to steal cars. Then, when you ditch the motor and run for it through people's back gardens, you'll be invisible to the thermal imaging cameras on the police helicopter.

Urinal Dockrat, Bucks

PAEDOPHILES. Confuse the police during questioning by making suggestive remarks about old ladies.

Johnny Pring, e-mail

POLICE. Save money on expensive sirens by putting a police dog on the roof of your patrol car and shutting the door on its tail before attending a 999 call.

Andy Bradshaw, e-mail

DISCOURAGE burglars by wearing a policeman's uniform and standing outside your house day and night.

C. Byker, Rotherhyde

HELP the local police by popping into the local mortuary every day to see if you can identify any of the bodies.

J. Lewis, Lichfield

POLICE officers on ITV's The Bill. Avoid giving suspect criminals a 100-yard head start by not shouting "Oi!" when you see them at that distance.

Berry, e-mail

HOMEOWNERS. Put an ancient Egyptian type curse on all your property. Then, if you are burgled and the police don't catch the culprit, you can rest assured they will die of a plague of boils or something.

P. Nevitt, Springwell

BEAT police speed traps by stopping your car every 200 yards and pretending to mess around under the bonnet. This way traffic cops will be unable to accurately record your speed for any length of time.

S. Daniels, Halifax

CASH-STRAPPED police forces. The average police woman's uniform costs around £250. But Ann Summers does a wipe-clean one for under £20. So save money and improve public relations in one stroke.

W. Walker, e-mail

SLOW traffic down in your street by getting your wife to dress as a policewoman and stand pointing a hairdryer at cars as they pass by.

R. Nest, Chippenham

GIVE off-duty policemen a taste of their own medicine by stopping them in the street and asking them where they're going.

C. Arrow, Norwich

REMAIN on your toes when driving by cutting out a picture of a police car and glueing it onto your rear view mirror.

Mr C. Savoury, Yeovil

CROOKLOCKS designed to secure car steering wheels can just as easily be fastened to a toilet seat, thus preventing burglars from using your lavatory.

J.B., Timperley

POLICEMEN. Why not walk up and down the street remarking to each other how the public are getting older every day.

D. Tucker, Chelmslow

Hughie Green's TOPPORTUNITY TIPS

IF being pursued by a rogue rhinoceros, run in a straight line directly away from the animal. Just before he catches you, dart quickly to one side or the other. Unable to stop or change direction, the bulky animal's momentum will carry him a good distance away, enabling you to run up a tree and call for help.

Mrs B. Sellers,
Cricklewood

DISPOSE of used toilet roll tubes in threes. Two can be compressed and then inserted into the other one to save space in the rubbish bin.

Mrs D. Park,
Bedlington

DURING cold weather a block of lard makes an inexpensive substitute for the more new-fangled modelling clays popular with children nowadays. And instead of being trodden into the carpet after use, it can be collected up and used to fry black pudding, etc.

K. McGrath,
Duns

A SMALL tree standing in the corner of the room and decorated with coloured lights, tinsel and baubles makes an ideal Christmas decoration.

H. Lovatt,
Reading

ALWAYS use the 'Five Items or Less' checkout at your local supermarket, no matter how many items you have in your trolley. Simply bring a group of friends shopping with you, and divide the contents of your trolley amongst them.

T. Parsnip,
Bolhamchestertonpoolwood

PAINT the windows of your car black to enjoy the benefits of night-time driving during the day.

P. Murray,
Hampstead

SURPRISE your teenage son by putting cigarettes instead of candles on his birthday cake. Everybody cheer as he lights his first one up.

Mrs E. Hawes,
Kettlebury

STOP visitors from using your phone without asking by taking it off the hook, and sitting on the receiver.

Nick Dwyer,
Brighton

CONVINCE people you are the new Messiah by taking a bottle of mineral water into the off licence and exchanging it for some cheap wine, buying a loaf of bread and some fish fingers at the corner shop, then getting your mates to nail you to a tree.

S. G.,
Wembley

RECORD the sound of your wife having an orgasm, and then listen to the tape through headphones next time you make love. That way you can have sex without waking her up.

Frank Wilson,
Southend

GIRLS. 'Roll your own' tampons using cigarette papers and a packet of cotton wool.

Graham Townend,
Shipley

MAKE mealtimes fun by dipping potatoes in food colouring before slicing and frying. Hey presto! Rainbow chips.

Mrs J. Crookes, Grantham

BY jogging to a restaurant behind a taxi my wife and I were able to save £5.80 in taxi fares last Saturday night.

N. Holland, Fareham

AMUSE your children by dressing as a clown and performing card tricks over breakfast.

I. Beadle, Dartford

FARMERS. Rid your land of 'New Age Travellers' by burning down the village Post Office. If they can't cash their giros, they'll soon move on.

S. Hanna, Liverpool

DONT waste money on expensive Swiss cheese. Just buy Cheddar, and poke holes in it with an old knitting needle.

G. Dent, Boscombe

LEFT over Christmas tree 'needle drop' spray can be used on pets to prevent them dropping hairs on the carpet.

P. Cherry, Avon

APPLY first aid to injured gingerbread men by dressing any cuts or scrapes in tagliatelle bandages.

Mrs L.H., Longhorsely

READ small print easily and without the use of expensive glasses by looking at it through a pint glass full of water.

E. C., Leeds

MAKE 'quiet' dice by compressing marshmallows into a cube shape, toasting them gently, and then painting dots on the side. Hey presto! The ideal gift for a deaf board games fan.

G. Banks, Stoke

SUCK the eyes from attacking zombies using a Black and Decker Dustbuster. The blinded ghouls will then wander aimlessly and can be dispatched at a more leisurely pace using the usual methods..

J. T., Thropton

MAKE your own orthopaedic car seat cover by threading conkers onto a string vest.

Mr G. Walton, Gosforth

ALWAYS keep a pound of lard in your pocket so that if you get your head stuck in railings you'll be able to grease your ears and slide out.

Kate Emblen, Uxbridge

DON'T throw away old pieces of string simply because they're too short. Knot them together and hey presto! A new, longer, useful piece of string.

Sam Evans, Shropshire

SAVE the price of a new television licence by simply keeping your old one and only watching repeats which you've already paid for.

S. Filler, Rochester

TIN foil custard tart dishes glued to your front bumper make cheap and economical replacements for expensive fog lamps.

L. Hall, Morpeth

NON-SWIMMERS. Fill a pair of goggles with water and put them on. Then dip your nose in a cup of water, and squirt water into both your ears with a water pistol. Hey presto! You're experiencing all the pleasures of swimming without the inconvenience or expense of travelling to your local pool.

Andrew Powell, Portsmouth

FINE tune your eye-hand co-ordination by trying to 'bomb' ants or similar crawling insects on the pavement on your way to work, using small ball bearings. Improve your accuracy each day by using smaller-sized ball bearings.

Tim, Romford

Green Cross Tips

VIDEO GAME enthusiasts. Black out your car windscreen and drive only using the SatNav display.

Sam Finch, e-mail

WOMEN drivers. When driving to work try getting out of bed ten minutes earlier than usual. This will enable you to put your make-up on using the bathroom mirror, and not in the rear view mirror of your car whilst sitting at a green traffic light.

A. Compass,
Red Leceistershire

LORRY drivers. Keep your indicator on for half an hour after each manoeuvre in order to keep us car drivers on our toes.

S. Macreary, Hollingworth

DRIVERS. Save money on tinted windows by setting a small fire in the glove compartment and allowing the plastic to burn long enough to deposit a thin layer of soot on the glass. Remember not to wind your windows down or it will come off.

Bazalini, e-mail

TAKE the trauma out of serious road traffic accidents by replacing your driver's airbag with a large Whoopee cushion. You'll still be laughing even while you're being cut from the wreckage.

Rob Hill, Wolverhampton

KNIGHT RIDER fans. Paint your Ford Sierra black and attach red fairy lights to the bonnet. Then drive to a gay bar and ask a particularly camp bloke to record a few words onto a cassette for you. Play it back as you're driving along, and hey presto! All the girls will mistake you for that lanky arsehole off Baywatch.

Hec & Ham, Dorset

LADY drivers. Draw a little diagram on a Post-it showing the position of the handbrake and gearstick, and stick it to your dashboard. This will save you having to look for them when the lights go green.

Barno, London

DRIVERS. Overcome boredom on motorway journeys by closing your eyes for as long as you dare, then daring yourself to close them for longer.

Tim Bradbury, Bristol

LORRY drivers. Save pounds by spending less on pornography and axes to kill women with.

Ian Corrigan, e-mail

WINDSCREEN covered in frost and late for work? Don't waste time scraping it off, simply drive around leaning out of your window like the woman in the Black A-Class Mercedes in rush hour traffic in Sedgley in the West Midlands.

Jonny Eye, e-mail

CAR drivers. Get away with not wearing a seat belt by painting a diagonal black stripe on all your shirts.

Andy Wright, e-mail

IF THE driver behind is too close, simply pull on the handbrake. This will not activate your brakelights and he will have no warning that you are about to stop. Watch his face in your rear view mirror as his car slams into the back of you.

D. Campbell, Cambridge (not the university)

WHILE out driving, try using this catchy rhyme to help remember what the different traffic lights mean. I find it most useful as I approach busy junctions.

When the red light does shine,
We must stop at the line.
When the amber is there,
We should all take good care.
But when the green light does show,
Then off we may go.

Mrs P. Madeley, Rawdon

MICRA drivers. The little number '5' on your gear-stick refers to what is known as 'fifth gear'. This will allow you to reach speeds of over 25 mph.

Rebecca, e-mail

LORRY drivers. Make time appear to stand still by attempting to overtake another lorry whilst taking care not to actually accelerate.

Errol Fudge, e-mail

MOTORISTS. Keep a small black sponge in your car. If you get pulled over by the police for using your mobile phone whilst driving, you can grab it and claim you were just cleaning the side of your face.

Paul Joyce, Barnsley

TAXI drivers. Remove the bulbs from your indicators in case you momentarily forget what you do for a living and inadvertently signal.

Aiden, e-mail

HGV drivers. When driving up hills, the 'crawler' lane is the one on the fucking left.

Mr. F.R.T., Cardiff

CONVINCE other motorists that you have air conditioning in your car by driving around on a hot day with all your windows closed and wearing a thick ski jacket.

David Green, e-mail

DRINK as much as you like on long haul flights and don't worry about being over the limit when you drive home from the airport - the time difference will have taken care of that.
J. Walker, Hemel Hempstead

WEIGHT watchers. Avoid that devilish temptation to nibble at the chocolate bar in the cupboard or fridge by not buying the fucking thing in the first place, you fat bastards.
Anthony Simcox, France

NOT having a TV, I spend my evenings watching a glass-fronted cabinet which I pretend is a television. Not only do I save on electricity, but my 'television' does not require a licence.
I. P. A., Liverpool

DYSLEXICS. Try deliberately spelling words wrongly. This way at least you have a chance of spelling them correctly.
Phil Wasley, Liverpool

STRETCH a piece of elastic and make marks at one inch intervals. Hey presto! A telescopic ruler which takes up little room in a handbag or pocket. By stretching it to different degrees you can easily convert it from imperial to metric measurements.
A. Kinloch, Harringay

IF you have an artificial leg make it unnoticeable by wearing long trousers.
Craig, Stonehaven

DON'T waste that carton of boiled rice left over from your takeaway meal. Colour the grains with felt tip pens to make slightly large and possibly toxic 'hundreds and thousands'.
Mr Beech, Braintree

LIKE a lot of your readers my wife and I enjoy wearing rubber during sexual intercourse. To prevent chafing we always cover ourselves liberally in baking powder. This also helps me 'rise' to the occasion.
S. Dulay, Middlesex

TAKE £100 with you every time you visit a cashpoint. If the machine refuses to give you any money, avoid embarrassment by pretending to remove this wad from the machine, then walk away smiling.
Waz, Liverpool

X-FILES fans. Create the effect of being abducted by aliens by drinking two bottles of vodka. You'll invariably wake up in a strange place the following morning, having had your memory mysteriously 'erased'.
Sam Neffendorf, Weybridge

PRETEND you're a giant panda by giving yourself two black eyes, eating bamboo shoots and refusing to have sex with your wife.
Mrs Di Uretic, Hong Kong

BY jogging to church behind a Rolls Royce, carrying my daughter on my back I was able to save £12 in car hire charges at her recent wedding.
N. Holland, Fareham

MAKE cheap but effective baby rattles by glueing a lollipop stick to an empty matchbox, then filling it with ten woodlice.
Ms. G. M. Dowd, Wigan

STARSKY

DON'T change your trousers simply because the pockets are full. Add extra pockets by suspending old socks from the belt loops.
V. Woodsford, Nottingham

CHEFS. When fixing together the pieces of a broken cake, dry pasta spirals make perfect 'screws'.
D. Turner, Canterbury

CAN'T find a dictionary? Ever thought of trying a telephone directory? They contain many useful words, like Cooper, Black and Smart, all of which are listed in alphabetical order.
R. Clayton, Arbroath

OFFICE managers. Encourage primeval 'hunter gathering' instincts among your staff by hiding nuts and berries around the office and encouraging the staff to 'forage' for their food at lunch time.
R. Villa, Argentina

TAKE a selection of your old vinyl records along with you next time you go to an overpriced pizza restaurant. Take examples of a '45' single, an old '78' and a '33' long playing album, and use them to demonstrate to the idiot waiter exactly what size pizza you require. When it arrives, check it against your record to make sure it's the right size.
M. Hepworth, Halifax

TRAVEL free on trains by looking like a bicycle and leaning against a wall in the corridor.
Scott Shaw, Hemel Hempstead

45

MAKERS of the Gillette Mach 3 razor. Save money by putting the blade that shaves the closest at the front and forgetting about the other two.

Orbish,
e-mail

WOMEN. Don't waste energy faking orgasms. Most men couldn't give a shit anyway and you could use the saved energy to hoover the house after you've been banged.

Lee Cawood,
Hull

MUMS. After your kids have mastered spelling with Alphabetti Spaghetti, buy a tin of the normal stuff so as they can practise joined-up writing.

Jay,
e-mail

INSECT PORNOGRAPHERS. Wasps make excellent 'shaven-haven' actors when making hardcore films for bees.

F Quimby,
Merseyside

HUSBANDS. Prevent stress build up by accepting that your wife is never going to suck your cock again and handing over your wallet so as she can go shopping.

Mrs Realistic,
Everywhere

REGIONAL TV news reporters. Make a report on a recently-bereaved person more poignant by getting them to leaf through a photo album and wistfully look through a patio window, just in case you think they can't remember the person they have lost.

Eric Glastonbury,
e-mail

FINCHLEY parkies. Putting a second 'No Ball Games' sign 8 yards (7.32m) to the left of the current one will save us having to use a jumper for a goalpost.

Anthony Reuben,
e-mail

WHEN cooking spaghetti, tie all the ends together. That way you can eat it in one long suck, eliminating the drudgery of washing up knives and forks.

Johnny Schott,
Hackney

PARTY HOSTESSES. Cactus plants make excellent buffet sausage dispensers if you've run out of grapefruits and cocktail sticks.

Mrs Wilton,
Rochdale

SMOKERS. Buy inflatable furniture. If you fall asleep whilst smoking, your ciggie will burn a hole in it and the escaping air will put it out.

Kerry Palmer,
Harlow

FELLAS. Avoid pissing on the lavatory floor during the night after an evening of heavy drinking by nailing a pair of slippers to the floor directly in front of the toilet. Later, when you roll out of bed and stagger into the bathroom, simply slide your feet into the slippers and voila! You're in the perfect position for a piss.

Mr I. Stadium,
Gateshead

PS. For bowking assume a kneeling position with your knees in the slippers.

FRUIT lovers. Wearing a top hat instantly solves the age old pineapple transportation problem.

Nisbet Crawford,
e-mail

IN THE same way that a lazy eye can be cured by covering the other eye with frosted glass, a lazy ear can be cured by pushing a cork into the good one.

D. C. Dry, Boston Spa

SINGLE men. Get a glimpse of married life by taping Woman's Hour on Radio 4, then playing it back at a higher volume than the TV whilst trying to watch something on Discovery Wings.

Graham Marsh,
e-mail

PAUL Daniels. Liven up your routine by actually sawing the 'lovely' Debbie McGee in half on stage.

Rollo Bin Web,
White City

AVOID wasting hot water by emptying the bath into a series of Thermos flasks and storing it until required again.
Mrs S. Ark, Gwent

DISGUISE unsightly power station cooling towers as elephants' feet by simply painting toenails on the bottom, and putting a giant 600 foot umbrella in the top.
Brian Johnson, Brighton

LADIES. A toilet freshener in your handbag helps keep it smelling fresh.
Jackie P., Bolton

FROZEN drop scones make handy coasters for hot drinks. By the time you finish your drink, the scones should have thawed and will be warm enough to add hot butter and jam.
N. Thorpe, Hockley

A SIMPLE pocket calculator placed alongside your television is a constant source of amusement. Watch your friends' faces as they try in vain to change the TV channel with it.
P. T., Aigburth

SAD blokes. When attempting to get into a barmaid's knickers, why not 'playfully' pull back your tenner just as she reaches to take it when paying for a round. It really turns me on.
Rosie, Bristol

AVOID waiting for a doctor's appointment by making one for 9.00am every morning. If you wake up feeling well, simply phone up and cancel it.
R. Dury, Ruddington

UNEMPLOYED people. Why not brighten up Christmas by glueing glitter around the edges of your UB40?
Nobby Board, Wall

PLAY 'McDonald's Drive Thru' with your kiddies by getting them to ride past the living room window on their tricycles and order what they want for tea. Then let them ride to the kitchen window where you hand them something completely different to eat. Unless they ordered fish fingers, in which case you tell them to park on the flower bed and wait for half an hour until they're ready.
J. McGovern, Nottingham

SMOKERS. Take the effort out of stubbing out cigarettes by placing a used, damp tea-bag at the bottom of your ashtray.
Chris Douglass, Stafford

HEAVY smokers. Don't throw away those filters from the end of your cigarettes. Save them up and within a few years you'll have enough to insulate your loft.
Mr J. Hedley, Northumberland

CONVINCE fellow train travellers that you're an off duty soldier by standing in the corridor at the end of the train drinking cans of beer. Add to the effect by occasionally falling out of the door to your death whilst the train is in motion.
Mrs Anne Field, Kirby

DEFUSE 'road rage' stand-offs by stretching out your arms and suggesting you both hug.
Austin Fisher, Finsbury Park

CUT laundry bills. Tie your dirty linen to your neighbour's roof rack next time he visits the car wash.
R. Hughes, Mid Glamorgan

CAN'T afford expensive tights? A pair of stockings stapled into a pair of underpants makes a cheap but effective alternative.
P. Melba, Onslow

WHEN shopping for a ruler or tape measure, always measure the one you intend to buy with another one before paying for it, thus ensuring that the measurements on the one you are buying are accurate.
Mr C. Bourbon, Hereford

MAKE the postman think you are sexually active by opening the door each morning looking tired, but grinning broadly.
Andrew Petrie, Kidderminster

CHEGGERS PLAYS TOP!

TIPS

Betty Driver's
HOT
POT
TOP
TIPS

PUT blue food colouring in your beer next time you visit the pub. Not only is your unusual drink a talking point, but the risk of your pint being stolen while you are at the toilet is greatly reduced.

B. Redesmouth,
Hawick

PUB LANDLORDS. Convince your customers that you are not an alcoholic by walking round with a mug of coffee for the first twenty minutes after opening.

Grant Warner,
New Zealand

FELLAS. Whenever you visit a pub with a male friend, wear a passport-sized photograph of your wife, cut into the shape of a heart, on your lapel in order to dispel any rumours that you might be homosexual.

L. Hall,
Newcastle

GENERATE virtual after-time drinking by simply setting your watch two hours fast and going to the pub two hours earlier. An added bonus is that when you arrive home pissed, yoiu can get two hours extra in bed by simply setting your watch back to normal.

Andy Hill
(Professor
of Drinking),
Kingswinford

PUB landords. Save money on posters and printing by having one huge sign that reads 'Big Screen Sports Here, No Smoking, Car Wash, Lease This Pub, For Sale.'

John Smith,
Nottingham

PRETEND your house is a pub by stubbing out cigarettes on the carpet, watering your cans of beer and kicking your wife out into the garden at 11.30.

Dave Upton,
Hereford

GIRLS in the pub. Don't sing or hum along with the jukebox. You sound shit and embarrass your boyfriend.

A. Smith,
Fulchester

PREVENT your ears from being bitten off in the pub by Sellotaping them flat to the side of your head.

P. Ash,
Kent

ALCOHOLICS. Don't worry where the next drink is coming from. Go to the pub, where a large selection is available at retail prices.

Ed Freeman,
e-mail

I REGULARLY drive to the pub, but am never guilty of drink-driving. The secret is to consume so much alcohol that by closing time you have completely forgotten ever owning a car.

Mike Grey,
Essex

PUB LANDLORDS. If you're trying to close for the night but Morrissey is refusing to drink up and leave, simply throw a plastic water bottle at his head and the big twat will storm off home in a huff within seconds.

L. Salisbury,
Inverness

MAKE visits to the dentists less nerve-wracking by popping into the pub first for five or six pints of beer.

T. Horswill,
Bedford

TAKE a roll of clingfilm to the pub. When it's your round, use it to cover the tops of the drinks, then carry them back from the bar in your pockets.

D. Porchester,
Rochester

John Craven's TIPSROUND

SILENCE your windy bottom by pulling apart your buttocks before you pump. Hey presto! No embarrassing 'fart' noise.

*P. Fletcher,
Wrexham*

CREATE your own 'boil-in-the-bag' cod in parsley sauce by scraping the breadcrumbs off a fish finger and placing it inside a used condom.

*E. Evans,
Evesham*

NEXT time you have a large family gathering such as a wedding or a birthday party, don't invite Angela Lansbury. If she does turn up, call the police, an ambulance and the coroner immediately.

*S. Hammer,
Bromsgrove*

AVOID soiling your trousers by not pulling apart your buttocks when you think you are about to fart.

*P. Fletcher,
Wrexham*

GRAFFITI artists. Don't forget to take a can of brick-coloured spray Tippex in case you make a mistake.

*Jonathan Morr,
Barnes*

AMERICAN organised crime leaders. Upon capturing the 'A' Team, do not under any circumstances lock them in a shed full of tools and useful scrap materials.

*Chris Jones,
Reading*

MAKE sex with your wife more exciting by telling her to wear lots of lipstick, and wash her mouth out with vodka. Then you can pretend you're shagging some old scrubber you've just picked up in a nightclub.

*F. Lair,
Kelso*

ANNOY traffic wardens by knocking their hats off.

*Mr I. Woods,
Bolton*

GIANT cigarettes can be made cheaply and easily using surplus household items. Simply pack lawn clippings inside a roll of old wallpaper, then pop an unused toilet roll in the end as a filter. You can light it using a giant match.

*G. Dawson,
Bletchley*

FEEL like a million dollars next time you arrive home by gluing Rice Krispies onto your car tyres. When you park it will sound as if you are rolling up on an expensive gravel drive.

*D. Treloar,
Wandsworth*

GET RID of irritating pieces of meat stuck between your teeth by popping a handful of maggots into your mouth and allowing them to crawl around your gums for a few minutes after each meal.

*I. Meatgone,
Nottingham*

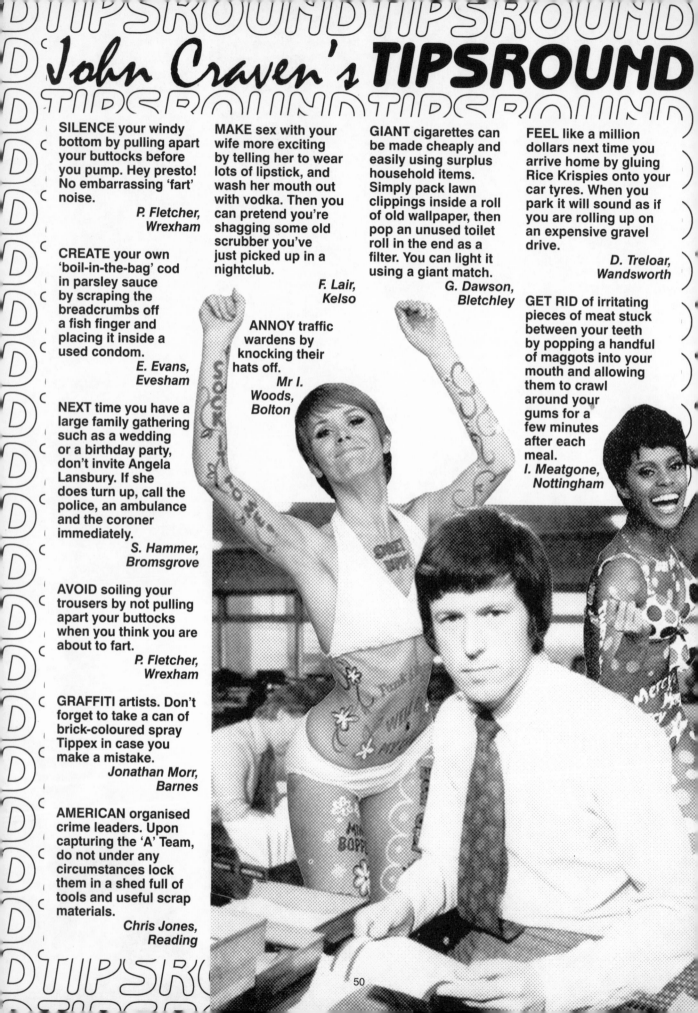

DON'T throw away used matches. Sharpened with a pen-knife, they are ideal for picking up small pieces of cheese, pineapple or cocktail sausages.

S. Jones, Edinburgh

AMERICAN locomotive drivers. When confronted with a car obstructing a rail crossing, the brake pedal is the one that slows the train down, not the one that sounds the fucking horn.

Jim Gearbox, Lamesville

DON'T waste money on expensive Cheddar cheese. Simply buy Swiss cheese and fill the holes with butter.

G. Dent, Boscombe

INTERNATIONAL master criminals. Tell your guards to shoot James Bond in the head at the first available opportunity. Under no circumstances give him a guided tour of your base, or leave him in the custody of attractive women in bikinis.

S. Stars, Welwyn

IMPRESS the neighbours' children by climbing onto your roof and then walking a couple of yards off the edge. Don't look down. Just bend down slowly, and tentatively probe the lack of 'ground' beneath you. Then stand up again, give a feeble wave, and plummet to the ground with a crash.

R. Runner, Arizona

a white laboratory coat, and parking a JCB digger outside your house for a few days. Then dim and flicker the lights in your house during the night and replace the JCB, unseen, with a Tonka toy of the same description. Watch their faces the next morning!

Prof. J. Francis, Rhondda

KEEP old light bulbs after they 'pop'. When your neighbour asks you to look after his house while he's away on holiday, swap them for some of his.

I. Legg, Lyndhurst

AN old television, with a toaster inside, makes a cheap but effective 'microwave' oven. For making toast.

W. M. Low, Lowick

GET into the cinema free of charge by looking bored, carrying an ice cream tray and wearing a silly hat.

Mrs D. Table, Hendon

STEREO too loud? Simply place the speakers inside a cupboard. The volume can then be easily controlled by opening and closing the cupboard doors.

L. Shumebottom, Market Drayton

RAM raiders. Make sure you use someone else's car when smashing into shop fronts. On a recent raid I netted goods worth over £1000, but the damage to my car came to £2,700.

A. Smith, Gateshead

PRETEND you've reached the 'Eliminator' stage on Gladiators by running the wrong way up an escalator in Marks & Spencers.

R.W., Merseyside

COAL MEN. Save having to wash your clothes by taking a night time job delivering sacks of flour.

J. R. Polley, Yeovil

CONVINCE neighbours that you have invented a 'shrinking' device by ruffling your hair, wearing

WELL-CHEWED bubblegum makes an ideal sealant for around baths, sinks and work tops, and works out only eight times the cost of conventional silicon-based sealants. Occasionally, pick it off and chew it during idle moments in order to prevent it from drying out.

D. Holst, Beckenham

OLD folk. Make mealtimes easier by employing a set of novelty clockwork teeth to pre-chew your food before it enters your mouth.

J. Tait, Thropton

DON'T waste hundreds of pounds having that tattoo of an ex-girlfriend's name removed from your arm by laser surgery. Simply give your new girlfriend £51 so she can have her name changed legally by deed poll to the one on the tattoo.

D. Kisilevsky, South Kensington

WHY pay the earth for expensive jigsaws? Just take a bag of frozen chips from the freezer and try piecing together potatoes.

B. Reastford, Ironville, Notts.

WHO said used tampons were useless? A spot of glue and half a tube of glitter transforms them into ideal Christmas tree decorations.

Christine Williams, Wimbledon

CONVINCE neighbours and any passers-by that you have fluorescent strip lights in your bedroom by rapidly flicking the switch on and off for a few moments every evening before you enter the room.

Mike Millar, Glasgow

TOBLERONE chocolate bars make ideal 'toast racks' for Ritz crackers.

Max China, Kendal

OFFICE workers. Position your fax machine up against your paper shredder. By aligning them carefully together you can save hours of needless paperwork by disposing of all incoming faxes the moment they arrive.

Paul Williams, Kennington Oval, SE 11

POP a few tea-bags into your hot water tank and you can make a hot cuppa anytime by simply turning on the hot tap.

Mrs M. Growitt, Birmingham

NOW that an increasing number of products are no longer tested on animals it makes sense to keep several household pets in order that you can carry out your own tests, as and when required.

Iris Pissier, Hull

PRETEND you have a fantastic sex life by bouncing up and down on your bed several times a day, moaning loudly. Then look at your neighbours' jealous faces every time you leave the house.

P. Pinto, Edgeware

TOE NAIL clippings, chopped up finely, make an ideal substitute for wood chippings when repairing wood chip wallpaper.

T. Marriage, Fulham

BEE keepers. Keep your hives in strawberry fields to get jam instead of honey.

D. Unwin, Highgate

AVOID getting fluff caught in your turn-ups by turning them down. Having done so the fluff will invariable gather elsewhere.

Z. Monkhouse, Gosforth

KING-sized Mars bars make ideal normal-sized Mars bars for giants.

T. Dell, Southampton

KEVIN KEEGAN'S FOOTBALL TIPS

FOOTBALL managers. As teams invariably play better when 'reduced to ten men', why not start the match with only five players? This way, if your team plays crap you can change the whole lot of them and still have your substitutes on the bench.
Dave Lee, Dorset

AN empty sardine tin makes an ideal miniature five-a-side pitch for teams of ladybird footballers. A grain of sugar rounded at the corners with a nail file makes a useful ball. But be sure to coat it with bleach or weed killer. Otherwise the ladybirds will eat it.
A. E. Greenall, Liverpool 11

DADS. Force your son to play football only using his left foot by cutting the front off his right boot. In a few years' time, when he's England's only left footed player, you can become his agent and retire.
G. Coad, e-mail

FOOTBALL teams. Fed up with good attacking play being let down by the final ball? Simply plan your moves to end one pass quicker and watch the goals fly in.
Steve Fitzpatrick, Birmingham

FOOTBALL managers. Force the opposition into committing foul after foul for dangerously high feet by fielding a team consisting entirely of dwarves.
Harry Perrin, e-mail

PROFESSIONAL footballers. Remember, there is plenty of time to get pissed after your playing career has ended.
T. Haines, London

MARK LAWRENSON. When the camera moves away from you in a wide shot on Football Focus, don't do that shifty sideways glance to see if you are still on screen as you get caught every time.
Mark Bates, e-mail

NIGHTCLUB owners. Cut out trouble in one fell swoop by simply banning professional footballers.
G. Lane, Bury

FOOTBALL fans with a lisp. Support Barcelona so as you can shout for your team without sounding stupid.
Welly Gogster, Kidsgrove

FOOTBALLERS. Pass the ball slowly amongst your defenders and goalkeeper during extra time and then moan about the 'insane lottery' of a penalty shootout.
Ryan Pooh, e-mail

ENJOY all the thrills and spills of professional football management by driving to a motorway service station with a friend and passing an envelope full of Monopoly money backwards and forwards under the table.
Brian & Alex, Thwaite

ARMCHAIR football fans. Create a real stadium atmosphere in your sitting room by sharing your armchair with two or three fat neighbours. Get your wife to sit on the floor in front of you, and tell her to stand up whenever anything exciting happens.
Pippa Legg, Lyndhurst, Hants.

FOOTBALL hooligans. Go to matches on horseback, dressed as Medieval knights, and challenge the mounted police officers to a jousting tournament.
A. Armitage, Penzance

CONVINCE the birds you're a top professional footballer by calling them a taxi, then pulling the door off when it arrives, and kicking the shit out of the driver.
Mr C. Bell, Manchester

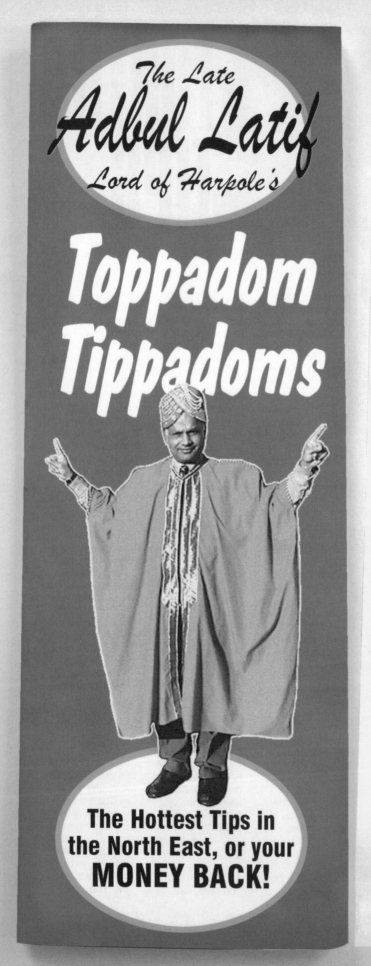

The Late
Adbul Latif
Lord of Harpole's

Toppadom Tippadoms

The Hottest Tips in the North East, or your MONEY BACK!

Tandoori Tips

LOST all the balls for your table football? Simply fill it with water and hey presto! - an exciting synchronised swimming game for all the family.

Andrew Smith, e-mail

KEEP your wife on her toes. Nail the housekeeping money to the ceiling.

S. Round, Paignton

TIE a fish on a piece of string, climb onto your neighbour's roof and dangle the fish in front of his window. He'll think his house is underwater.

R.R., Kent

Rice Tips

AVOID bickering and petty arguments by immediately punching anyone with whom you disagree.

S. Taylor, Watford

RATHER than carry shopping bags around with me or pay for expensive supermarket carrier bags, I always eat my groceries at the checkout. Not only does this save pounds on carriers, but it has also reduced my gas bill.

Anne Brookes, Warrington

CAN'T play the piano? Then entertain party guests with a comical impression of snooker star Dennis Taylor, by simply wearing your glasses upside down!

B. Potter, Aberdeen

Sundry Tips

PLACE dead goldfish inside library books and slam the books shut. The squashed fish will serve as useful bookmarks, and are doubly handy as their smell will act as a reminder that the books are due for return.

Doris Franklin, Weymouth

ON hot summer nights, keep cool in bed by using a hot water bottle filled with liquid nitrogen.

Snowplough, Cambridge

Chef's Special Tips

IF your brakes fail whilst driving at speed, release your bonnet catch. The raised bonnet will provide vital wind resistance and help slow down the vehicle.

V. Ground, Hartlepool

AVOID embarrassment after tripping in the street by repeating the same movement several times to make it seem like part of your normal behaviour.

B. Sweeny,
Cove Road

MOUNTAIN bikers. Stop that irritating squeal from your brakes and reduce wear on them by oiling the rims of your wheels before taking on that tricky descent.

S. S.,
Bunny

PLACE the candles evenly around the surface of a frozen Birthday cake. Lighting them early will help defrost it in time for your party.

Mrs J. Thomas,
Ryegate

DAB a series of dots onto bourbon biscuits with icing, and voila! Edible dominoes.

B. Thompson,
Houston

PREVENT sneak thieves from stealing the 'crooklock' from your car by attaching one end to the steering wheel and the other to one of the floor pedals.

D. Marshall (Mr),
Stockton-on-Tees

DON'T throw away those old car batteries. Placed inside an old pillow case they make an ideal counter balance on a see-saw.

Alex,
Burnley

RAVERS. Pop a wooden spoon in your mouth when dancing. This will eliminate the risk of biting off your tongue in the event of an epileptic fit caused by strobe lighting and will soon become a fashion item.

W. Brooks,
Somerset

SPECTACLE wearers. Avoid the nuisance of low-flying military aircraft by sticking strips of brown parcel tape across the top half of your lenses.

J. Lofts,
Chiswick

DON'T waste money on expensive firelighters. Use potato peelings instead. If they don't ignite at first, leave them in an airing cupboard to dry for a few days.

Mr. Sark,
Derby

the second to reveal your pet's weight. (If weighing goldfish, remember to make an allowance for the weight of the bowl and the water).

Rob Keith,
Nottingham

MAKE your own matches by painting a pea red, soaking it in petrol overnight, then pronging it on the end of a cocktail stick.

G. Dawson,
Bletchley

VICARS. When asked why Almighty God permits so much suffering in the world, always couch your answers in flowery, poetic prose which sounds wise and meaningful but in actual fact means fuck all. Phrases like "all part of a greater plan" and "the path of life is many forked" always come in useful.

Ann Atheist,
Whitley Bay

PREVENT rice from sticking together by boiling each grain separately. Use several saucepans simultaneously to speed up the process.

David Dinsdale, Warley

STYLISH mirrored sunglasses can be made using two milk bottle tops and some pipe cleaners, saving pounds on similar items sold in trendy shops.

Rick Glover,
Malaysia

WEIGH your pet by first of all weighing yourself, then weighing yourself again, this time carrying your pet. Deduct the first weight from

MAKE the bin man think your dustbin is a dead dalek by placing it upside down and filling it with water and Alka-Seltzer tablets. Then stand behind your back yard door, with crocodile clips attached to your testicles, saying "exterminate' and "out of control" over and over again.

E. S. Batey,
Walsall

BARRY SHEENE

TRAFFIC cops. Don't waste time and money installing video cameras in your c ars. Install them in the front and rear windows of all Volvo 340s and Maestros driven by old age pensioners. That way all the accidents which the doddering old fogies cause will be recorded on tape.

**Andrew Davies,
Yarm**

CAN'T **afford a video? Lie a toaster sideways on the floor beneath your television. Friends will never know the difference.**

S. Winstanley,
Orrel

ARCH villians of Gotham City. Should the opportunity present itself, kill Batman and Robin using traditional techniques (gun, knife, etc.) rather than leaving them unattended at the mercy of some untested 'Heath Robinson'-style killing machine of your own design.

**C. Gordon,
Gotham City P.D.**

FOOL **dinner guests into thinking you have woodworm in the house by drilling small holes in the arms and legs of your dining chairs.**

S. Cooper,
Tring

MAKE rowing a boat easier by drilling a few large holes through the oars.

**John Tait,
Thropton**

BLINK **alternately with one eye and then the other whilst watching TV soaps. This way you'll never miss a second. If you add it all up you probably miss up to an hour of your favourite programmes each year due to normal blinking.**

J. Pears,
Wimbledon

LEEDS United fans. Save time on a Saturday afternoon by just popping along to Elland Road for the last two minutes of each game, as this is invariably when all the action is.

**T. Hennesey,
Nottingham**

GIVE **friends the impression that you wear contact lenses by blinking frequently midway through conversations, and stopping to carefully pull at your lower eyelids.**
Michael Hudson,
Bingley

WHEN travelling by bus, always take a polaroid photo of the queue so that when the bus arrives any arguments about people 'pushing in' can easily be settled.
R. Holmes, Putney

OLD LADIES. Worried some poor sod who's late for his bus is going to get past you on the pavement? Simply wander aimlessly from left to right. That will stop them.
Mark Giddings, Bristol

BUS drivers. Increase the number of people who believe you when you cite traffic as an excuse for your late arrival by not stopping halfway through a route to exchange a racist joke with a passing colleague.
Dan B, e-mail

COMMUTERS. When you leave your house, sprint the first 200 yards and then revert back to your regular walking speed. This will save you from having to do the run of shame for the bus nearer the stop and look like a fool when you miss it.
Micky the Lips, e-mail

On the

BUS drivers. Let every-one see how pig ugly your dog of a girlfriend is by letting her stand next to whilst you are driving, as if she owns the bus.
Mark Harris, Smegmaville

PENSIONERS. Get to the bus stop 30 minutes before your bus pass starts. That way you can spend half an hour whingeing that the driver wouldn't let you on the bus. You will especially enjoy this if the driver is black.
Simon Drugs, Walsall

CAR commuters. Experience the thrills and spills of running to catch a bus by dashing from your car into the house after work only to see your wife slowly carrying the TV set away into the next room.
C. Paper, Tunbury

BY jogging to work behind the bus I am able to save 96p a day in bus fares.
N. Holland, Fareham

PRACTISE being a paramedic by standing on the top deck of a bus, holding old ladies' hands and telling them "everything's going to be alright".
J. Edwards,
Staffordshire

COMMUTERS. Make the bus come quicker by standing by the corner looking for it coming down the road, then running back to the bus stop.
John Altree,
Hounslow

BUS drivers. Before complaining about them not having the right change, ask the passenger who has just boarded your bus if he or she would mind walking to the back window to see whether or not it is clear for you to pull out again from the bus stop. If it isn't you can then pull out anyway, causing cars to brake sharply, whilst at the same time sending the passenger sprawling as they attempt to make their way back down the bus.
R. Kerr,
Sunderland

BRIGHTEN up dull bus journeys by sitting in the middle of the back seat and saying "Take her away, warp factor six Mr Bus Driver" just before the bus pulls away from each stop.
Dominic Gartland,
Consett

DON'T waste electricity by flashing your headlights to invite buses to pull out in front of you. They invariably do so anyway.
H. Attwell,
Enfield

AVOID being engaged in polite conversations with strangers on buses by pretending to be drunk.
Trevor Williams,
Woolwich

BUS drivers. Pretend you're an airline pilot by wedging your accelerator pedal down with a heavy book, securing the steering wheel with some old rope, and then strolling back along your bus chatting casually to the passengers.
Mrs Joyce Clooney,
Littlehampton

WHEN boarding a bus, routinely try to avoid paying your fare by claiming you are with the person in front of you.
I. Peters,
Gravesend

TOP CAT TIPS

CONVINCE visitors you are a cat lover by taking a razor blade to your furniture and urinating frequently behind your settee.

B. Moore,
London E 17

SCABS with tufts of fur attached removed from your cat make ideal fishing flies.

D.T.,
Cardiff

POTHOLERS. Take a tip from cats and avoid getting stuck in holes by growing a moustache to the exact width of your body.

Ryan Lloyd,
Rhyl

SMARTIES tubes pushed over cats' legs make for a futuristic 'space cat'. For a really space-age look, cover the tubes in tin foil as well as your pet's tail. This also works with small dogs and the middles out of kitchen rolls.

Dominic Rickard,
e-mail

DISCOURAGE pigeons from sitting on your roof by tethering a cat to the TV aerial.

Roger Radio,
Feversham

PET OWNERS. Rats make ideal 'large print' mice for short-sighted cats.

Matthew Phillimore,
e-mail

CATS can be very costly in food and vet's bills. Save a fortune by simply not having a cat, and slashing your own furniture with a Stanley knife.

Bar Steward,
e-mail

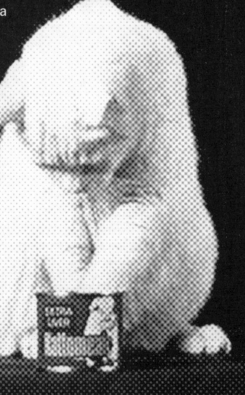

GIVE passers-by the impression that you own a cat by littering your garden with decapitated sparrows and sawing a hole in the bottom of your back door.

B. Moore,
London E 17

FIND out how many of your cat's lives are remaining by hitting it repeatedly with a mallet. The number of strokes required to bring about its demise will correspond with the number of lives that remained.

Mr G. Stone,
Brighton

CAT owners. Convince neighbours that you own a racing cat by putting a dish cloth over its back, wearing binoculars round your neck, and leading it in circles around your lawn.

Mrs Wm. Holland,
Stanton-in-Leak

SODA-SYPHON owners. The little green gas bottles are ideal for re-enacting the final scene from Jaws with your cat.

Charlie Farnsbarns,
e-mail

CAT owners. Save money on expensive cat carriers. Simply tie your pet's tail to one of its back legs to make a handy carrying loop.

Shelly Goblin,
e-mail

TREAT your cat by placing a mouse in a matchbox and feeding it on milk powder. Hey presto! 'Veal' mice.

B. Labone,
Kirby

WEATHER men. Save a fortune in meteorological expenses by simply saying that the weather will be the same as it was the day before. More often than not you'll be right.

P. Beading,
Cleveland

SIAMESE twins. A padded 'Ultrabra' makes a handy pair of skateboarding safety helmets.

B. McMahon,
Edinburgh

SPERM makes ideal 00-gauge tadpoles for model railway ponds.

D. Grear,
e-mail

BEAT the credit card companies at their own game by running up massive-bills on your credit cards and then killing yourself before your statements arrive, thus avoiding re-payment.

D. Payne,
Middlesex

EXPERIENCE the luxury of staying in a top hotel by keeping your fridge in the bedroom, filling it with chocolate, peanuts and drinks, and then burning a twenty pound note every time you eat or drink anything.

S. Park,
Wimbledon

READERS with old or perished hot water bottles may, after filling, wish to leave the problem bottle in the sink or bath and so reduce the risk of damp bedclothes.

Mr P. Jopling,
Bracknell

MAKE people in the pub think you're a doctor by carrying a small leather bag and not laughing at the words 'penis', 'clitoris' or 'scrotum'.

P. C.,
Leicester

IMAGINE you're in London by simply sitting in your car all day with the engine running, occasionally honking your horn, and never actually going anywhere.

G. Foster, Blyth

WHEN boiling an egg in the morning, save time by popping a tea bag and a drop of milk into the saucepan. Hey presto! A boiled egg and a ready-made cup of tea.

Hapag Lloyd,
Runcorn

MAKE neighbours think you've had a house fire by blackening your windows with shoe polish and throwing your mattresses out into the garden.

F. Lee,
Manchester

HOUSEWIVES. When making hubby's sandwiches for work, always fill one with toothpaste. Make sure he eats this one last, for healthier teeth and gums.

M. Bike,
Berkshire

STOP squirrels and birds taking food from your bird table by placing the food inside a biscuit tin, and securing the lid with heavy duty tape.

P. Reaney,
Rothwell

MOTORISTS. Enjoy the freedom of cycling by removing your windscreen, sicking half a melon skin on your head, then jumping red lights and driving the wrong way up one-way streets.

Maurice Traveller,
Brentford

FURTHER depress the owners of unprofitable and rapidly-failing tacky seaside gift shops by crossing the road purposefully in their direction, before veering off at the last moment.

Anon.,
Shanklin, I.O.W.

PLANE passengers. Always volunteer to sit next to that portly passenger who is having difficulty fitting into his or her seat. If the plane crashes in snow covered mountains you can survive for months by eating the blubbery bastard.

G. Hose,
Shed

On Tip of ♡ ♡ the World

TRUE TOP TIP ROMANCE

Following a blow to the head, Gary Rudd lost the ability to talk sense and could only repeat Top Tips. Desperate to save their relationship, his girlfriend Sonia Bream did the same. But it was putting a strain on their relationship...

A SHEET of sandpaper makes a cheap and effective substitute for costly maps when visiting the Sahara desert.
A. T. Loveday, Ramsgate

TRY painting a red cross at the bottom of your tea cups. When this becomes visible, your cup will be empty and you may wish to consider a refill.
Mrs I. Docherty, Carlisle

COLLECT your farts in sandwich bags during the winter. Store them in a safe place, and come summer these handy 'pump packets' will make ideal firelighters for barbecues etc.
Andy Rogers, Fenham

Sonia went to chat with her best friend, Sally. But when she got to Sally's flat, she was in for a big surprise...

AN even sprinkling of flour will lighten up the colour of your carpet. If you don't like the new shade, no problem. Simply vacuum if off.
C. Jones, Reading

HANG brussels sprouts on the end of a piece of string. Hey presto! Edible Christmas decorations for the kids.
Mrs I. Jones, Hebden Bridge

SPEED up darts games by attaching a length of string to each dart. After throwing, a sharp tug on the string will return your darts to you.
Patrick Matthews, Bolton

KEEP a hammer close to your bed in case any nails fall out of the ceiling at night.
Nick Dwyer, Brighton

RIGHT-handed people. Perform everyday tasks with your left hand, so that if you get a splinter you'll be able to carefully remove it with your right hand.
A. Pryde, Bromley

MAKE your neighbour think you're an alien by wrapping yourself from head to foot in tinfoil and standing in your garden late at night pointing at the stars, and making silly, high-pitched 'bleeping' noises.
Mrs B. Mirellees, March

RACE 'homing goldfish' by flushing them all down the lavatory. Leave all your taps running and see which one returns first.
J. King, Oswestry

OLD telephone directories make ideal personal address books. Simply cross out the names and address of people you don't know.
Mrs K. Smith, Bristol

The following evening, Sonia and Gary settled down for a quiet night in...

AN XR3i Cabriolet with the roof down makes a perfect roller skate for dinosaurs.
Dale Wadman, Leics

FREEZE loaves of bread, then sculpt them into animal shapes using a hammer and chisel. Once they've thawed, hey presto! Tasty animal bread zoo figures for the kids.
Mrs J. Crooks, Grantham

A BANANA skin makes an ideal sun hat for a star fish.
G. Hurst, New Cross

GIRLS. Make sure you don't miss out on a tan this summer. Go topless at the first hint of sunshine.
Rob Walker, Harrow

FOIL pick pockets by placing a freshly toasted 'Pop Tart' in each pocket. Would-be thieves will quickly rupture the fragile pastry and receive nasty finger burns from the steaming hot jam inside.
P. Turner, Liverpool

GIVE your goldfish a love-bite by inserting a straw into its bowl and sucking gently at its neck.
W. B. Levit, Hull

AT WEDDINGS make sure all the guests wear a paper hat with their names clearly written on the front. This will enable you to identify old faces from the past when viewing the pictures in years to come.
Ken Road, Luton

SAVE money on expensive nicotine gum by chewing ordinary gum and smoking a cigarette at the same time.
H. Cavendar, Kingston

OLD contact lenses make ideal 'portholes' for small model boats.
F. Johnson, Seaham

Suddenly...

WINKLE shells make ideal turbans for field mice requiring an exotic look.
John Tait, Thropton

BRIDES. Take no chances on your wedding day. Place marshmallows under your wedding cake to help it withstand any minor earthquakes or tremors.
D. Puttnam, Ryhope

HOUSEWIVES. When driving to the shops, always carry a stiff broom in the boot of your car. Use it to sweep the broken glass to the side of the road every time you have a minor accident.
D. Stammers, Canvey Island

Continued on page 97.

TELEPHONE salesmen. Increase company profits by reversing the charges whenever you call a customer. Invariably they'll accept the call, thinking it may be a relative in distress.

A. F.,
London

THIS summer, make snow for the kids by rubbing ice from your freezer compartment on a cheese grater.

Mrs R. Tea,
Stafford

REDUCE the risk of burns by making tea using cold water. Then heat the pot in the microwave.

William Doughty,
Bangkok

SINGLE mothers. A life-sized cut-out of Cecil Parkinson in your kitchen will act as an ideal male role model for your disadvantaged children.

R. On,
Haringey

CREATE the atmosphere of a top Soho sex club in your own home by getting your wife to remove her top and bring you a bottle of cheap champagne, then return ten minutes later with a bill for £500.

S. Park,
Wimbledon

DENTISTS. Why pay over the odds for a fancy hydraulic chair? Simply strap patients to an ordinary wooden chair suspended from the ceiling on elastic rope. Lower or raise the patient to the required position by skilfully positioning weights in their various pockets.

J. K.,
New Maiden

LEAVE your headlights on whenever you park your car in a large car park. If you are unable to find it on your return, simply go away again and come back when it has got dark.

M. Ross,
Peckham

HOLLOWED-out ravioli shells make ideal mittens for gingerbread men.

Mrs L. H.,
Longhorsley

IGNORE signs in hotel bathrooms telling you to put the shower curtain inside the bath. It takes 28 minutes to get the hooks off.

J. B. Cartland,
Brighton

WHEN parking in car parks, always carry a spare battery in the boot of your car in case the other one has gone flat by the time you eventually find your car.

M. Ross,
Peckham

BLIND people. Avoid getting dog shit on the end of your white stick by rolling a condom over the end. After a walk unroll the dirty condom and throw it in the bin.

Gary 'Carpet',
Axminster

DON'T buy expensive 'ribbed' condoms, just buy an ordinary one and slip a handful of frozen peas inside it before you put it on.

D. Duckham,
Didford

DENNIS NILSEN

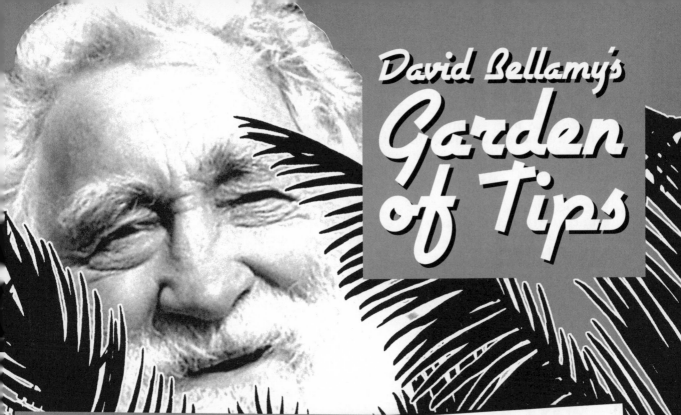

David Bellamy's Garden of Tips

CUT a kitchen chair in half, nail an old floorboard between the two pieces and you have a cheap and attractive garden bench.

A. Harmer, Frodsham

A HANDY gardening tip I learnt from my father is to build a fence or wall in between your garden and that of your neighbour. This wall or fence then provides an invaluable indication of where your garden ends and your neighbour's begins.

A. P., Bridlington

TRANSFORM your garden into a 'EuroDisney'-style theme park by charging your neighbour £20 to get in, £10 for an ice cream, and then making him wait four hours for a ride on your lawn mower.

S. Tempest, Plymouth

DON'T sell that old car for scrap. Park it outside your house, remove the engine and fill the gap with soil and flowers. Hey presto! An instant garden.

Dave Mullahev, Liverpool

INCREASE the size of your garden by moving the fence several feet into your neighbour's garden during the night.

R. Hope, Timperley

GARDENERS. Save money during the summer months by plugging your electrical lawn mower into your next door neighbour's electricity supply.

R. Hope, Timperley

GARDENERS. Save time cutting your lawn by using a strimmer. Simply pull the cord out to about 20 feet in length, start the strimmer and jump out of the way. Hey presto! a 40 foot diameter lawn cut in seconds. (This works best with circular lawns).

Rob Coxon, Sheffield

PILE litter neatly around your garden during the autumn. The bright colours are virtually indistinguishable from flowers during the winter months, especially if viewed whilst squinting, or from a great distance.

Mrs G. Richardson, Oxford

ACQUIRE the coolest garden in your street by placing Rayban sunglasses on your gnomes and replacing their fishing rods with small toy shotguns.

N. Aitchison, Nicosia, Cyprus

EDGE your lawn into the shape of a pair of trousers, then mow it in lines so that from above it looks like a giant pair of corduroy pants. Pockets can easily be added by planting small flower beds.

Hapag Lloyd, Runcorn

AVOID backache from bending to pick your tomatoes. Simply dig a trench four feet deep alongside your plants. Step into the trench and you'll find your tomatoes are conveniently at chest height.

John Tagliarini, Sicily

TURN your greenhouse into a garden shed by boarding up the windows with spare floorboards.

S. T., Pontefract

DON'T throw away old string vests. Nailed to the walls outside they make an excellent trellis for climbing plants.

A. Titmarsh, Harrogate

A SIMPLE plant pot, upturned on the top of your head, is ideal for doing comedy impressions of the late **Tommy Cooper**. Just like that!

R. Alderson,
Nantwich

PSYCHICS. Take advantage of electric night storage heating. Simply predict the next day's weather correctly, 24 hours in advance, every single day and, hey presto! A perfectly heated house every morning.

M. Barr,
Gloucester

HOUSEWIVES. I find the best way to get two bottles of washing-up liquid for the price of one is by putting one in your shopping trolley and the other in your coat pocket.

Mrs Smith,
Chester

MAKE shopkeepers feel like criminals and conmen by carefully checking their change, and holding bank notes up to the light before accepting them.

Dodswon,
Leicester

TOP UP your car battery with lemon juice. Not only does it have a high acid content, it will add 'zest' to your engine's performance and leave your exhaust fumes smelling lemon fresh.

W. Sill,
Frome

ALWAYS allow bald people to go in front of you in lavatory queues, as the loss of hair and onset of incontinence are usually simultaneous in middle-aged men.

A. Adderstone,
Bemerside

SAVE on charity donations by spending a pound on clothes at a charity shop, then selling them for 50p to another charity shop. This way you can give twice as much, at half the cost. I think.

Mrs A. Parker,
Notts.

WHEN throwing someone a sharp instrument such as a Stanley knife, or bread knife, always throw it blade first as they invariably tend to turn whilst in the air.

W. Stannier,
Cricklewood

MAKE firelighters by steeping white nougat overnight in your petrol tank.

B. Baxter, Potters Bar

REPAIR broken light bulbs by replacing the old glass with a partly inflated white balloon. Put it in the freezer to make it go hard.

K. Black,
Alnwick

HITCH-HIKERS. Improve your chances of getting a lift by not dressing up as a hunt saboteur and waving half a cardboard box at passing motorists.

John Kean,
London SE1

ELECTRICAL retailers. Deter ram raiders by

putting mirrors in your windows, causing criminals to swerve at the sight of their own car, thus hitting the shop next door.

R. Jar,
Tottenham

PREVENT your cold from spreading by placing a stout paper bag over your head. When you're finished with it, get rid of germs by spraying inside the bag with fly killer. The bag can then be re-used.

S. Evans,
Ruddington

SHOPKEEPERS. If the electrical retailer next door puts mirrors in his window, check your insurance cover in case a car swerves and crashes into your shop.

R. Jar,
Tottenham

A STRIP of black cardboard about two inches wide, worn over the eyes, makes a perfect disguise for Lottery or Pools winners wishing to conceal their identity.

Mark Anderson,
West Hampstead

DON'T buy Fairy Liquid. With the money you save from one bottle you'll be able to afford a meal in a restaurant, and someone else will do the dishes for you.

B. Jones,
Biddlecombe

HOW TIPS

CONVINCE friends and neighbours that you have a high-powered job in the City by leaving for work at 6am every morning, arriving home at 10 at night, never keeping social appointments, and dropping down dead at the age of 36.

S. James, Barnes

IN hot weather attach a length of string to a homing pigeon's leg and tie the other end to your ceiling rose. The bird will try to fly home, but instead will simply circle the room, creating a cooling breeze with its constantly flapping wings. Place breadcrumbs and water on a stepladder in the middle of the room so that it can stop occasionally for a rest and some refreshment.

Mr N. Bus, Haymarket

TEENAGERS. If a shopkeeper refuses to sell you cigarettes because you don't look old enough, take him to the nearest bus stop. When a bus comes, ask the driver for a child's fare. When he says you don't look young enough, leave the pair of them to argue about it, while you go back to the shop and steal the fucking cigarettes.

Russell Whyte, Dundee

WHEN buying a computer make sure you get 'state of the art' equipment by asking the man who delivers it to take it back and change it for the new model that has invariably superseded it during the two weeks in which you were waiting for it to arrive.

R. Daltrey, Gosforth

THREAD a long length of string through everything that you have in your home. Whenever you misplace something, simply follow the string from beginning to end and eventually you'll come across the missing item.

E. Tupp, Glamorgan

KEEP postie on his toes by making six defferently-shaped letterboxes in your front door (square, circle, star, rectangle, etc) and posting yourself six correspondingly-shaped parcels for him to deliver.

M. Cooper, Leyland

SURPRISE your wife by tidying her underwear drawer when she's out. Try on stockings to check for ladders, and try on bras and suspenders to check for broken clasps. Keep defective lingerie hidden in the shed as it can be used to clean up paint or tie garden canes, etc.

R. Leigh, Rayleigh

CATCH a condor by simply building a wooden stockade 1 metre high and 50 metres in diameter, and placing a dead goat in the centre. The bird will land inside the stockade to feed on the goat, but will then be unable to get out. This is because Condors require a run-up of at least 100 metres before they can gain the momentum necessary for take off.

G. Hill, Birmingham

ASK double glazing contractors to fill your new sealed window units with water and desiccated coconut. Rapidly opening and closing the windows will then create an instant 'snowstorm' effect.

H. Head, Wooler

KEEP losing the end of the Sellotape? Then why not coat it in sugar? When you need to use it simply lick off the sugar, use the tape, and then re-coat the new end.

G. Davis, Herts.

FELLAS. Play 'Rodeo Sex' by shagging your missus 'doggy fashion' and then calling her another bird's name. See how long you can stay on for!

Karin Love, Nottingham

IF a small child is choking on an ice cube, DON'T panic. Make the child drink as many hot drinks as possible, such as tea or coffee, and within minutes the blockage will have simply melted away.

Mrs F. Kippling, Swansea

CYCLISTS. Always carry with you a tin bath and about four or five gallons of water in plastic containers. In the event of a flat tyre this will enable you to locate any punctures you may have.

Andy Hodgson, Manchester

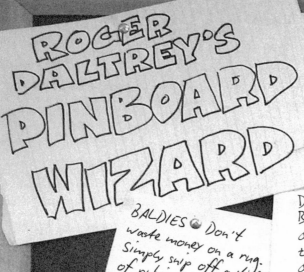

ROGER DALTREY'S PINBOARD WIZARD

[S]AVE hot water by going [t]o bed at 6.30 with a hot [wa]ter bottle. Get up an [ho]ur later and the water [will] still be hot enough for a [good] shave.

Mike Haworth,
Manchester

PEOPLE whose surn[ame] is Toblerone should always take along an empty Toblero[ne] chocolate box when a[t]tending interviews [for] office jobs. This woul[d] save your potential employer the expe[nse] of having to make [a] name triangle for your desk and there[by] increase your chance[s] of getting the job.

Mike Haw[orth]
Manch[ester]

BALDIES. Don't waste money on a rug. Simply snip off a tuft of pubic hair and glue it to the palm of your hand. Then every time you stroke your shiny head it will feel hairy.
S. Sheppard, Ipswich

DON'T waste money buying Big Country's Greatest Hits album. Simply buy one of their singles and play it over and over again.

Paul Goss,
Basildon

GIRLS. When applying cosmetics in a mirror, place a second mirror on a table behind you. Look over your shoulder in the first mirror to see yourself reflected in the second mirror in order to see what your make-up will actually look like to others, rather than the usual reversed image which you see in a single mirror.
J. Sulzer,
Ipswich

BEARDED MEN CAN OBTAIN THE APPEARANCE OF AN UPPER CLASS ARCTIC EXPLORER BY SIMPLY APPLYING TIPPEX TO THEIR BEARDS, PAINTING THEIR NOSES BLUE AND CUTTING OFF A COUPLE OF TOES. IT NEVER FAILS TO IMPRESS THE GIRLS.
BEN COLLINS, GALASHIELS

BATTENBURG cake, cut into 16 slices then arranged into a square, makes an ideal emergency chess board.
Graham Carter,
Ashford, Middlesex

CREATE a more relaxing atmospher[e in] your fridge by insta[ll]ing a dimmer switch.
Roger Ra[ ]
Favers[ham]

ILLEGAL immigrants. Convince people that you're Scottish by drinking whisky, wearing women's clothes and a ginger wig, and throwing big logs around your back garden.
Jock McPateli,
Stenhousemuir

ALWAYS put Pay and Display parking tickets upside down and in the centre of your windscreen in the hope that the parking warden will crick his neck trying to read it.
S. Lyall,
Dundee

neopost
BURY DRUMMER
3.00 pm!!

ACTION MEN EMBEDDED IN GRAPEFRUIT HALV[ES] MAKE EXTRA LARG[E] SUBBUTEO FOOTBALLERS SUITA[BLE] FOR ADULTS.
I.C. [ ]
GRIMSBY

WHEN going to the toilet I find it both easier and more pleasant if I remove both my trousers and my underpants before sitting down.

F. Carruthers, Derby

Deter your canary from flying around its cage by placing bulldog clips on both of its wings.

M. Faraday, Barking

FIND out what you look like when you're asleep by learning astral projection, and then glancing over your shoulder just as you are leaving your body.

Steve Wright, Hornsey

MAKE a giant 'high tar' cigarette by rolling up bark chippings in a roll of roofing felt, and not adding a filter.

G. Dawson, Bletchley

PRETEND you're listening to Radio One on long wave by slightly off-tuning the FM frequency and then wrapping the radio in a sleeping bag.

H. Clayton, Gateshead

FELLAS. Missus driving you up the wall? Make two pin pricks in your neck, then kill her with a mallet and a sharp piece of wood. Instead of arresting you, the cops will congratulate you for killing a vampire.

D. J. Bowen, Cardiff

N TIQUE
op owners. C
ate the ag
- old tables
sawing off
e of the legs
counting th
mber of rings
the woodgrain
his works for
airs too.

A. Sapling, Sevenoaks

PUT one-inch strips of masking tape across the top and bottom of your TV screen. Then, with the room lights switched off, watch your favourite programmes through binoculars. It's just like being at the cinema

Mrs. D. Parker, Boddingham

METAL washers make delicious Polo mints for sweet-toothed robots.

Miss J. Fisher, South Shields

Chris Poulton Knutsford

TV viewers. Avoid laziness by screwing your TV remote control to a wall or a piece of furniture at least ten feet away from your chair.

Hapag Lloyd, Runcom

PILE bricks at one end yous bath and it will require much less hot water to fill it up

James Lowe Nottingham

GIRLS. Next time you feel like throwing a ball over-arm, don't do it, because you can't and it just looks silly. Just throw it girlie under-arm style, and no-one will laugh at you, or get hurt.

D. Thresher, Wapping

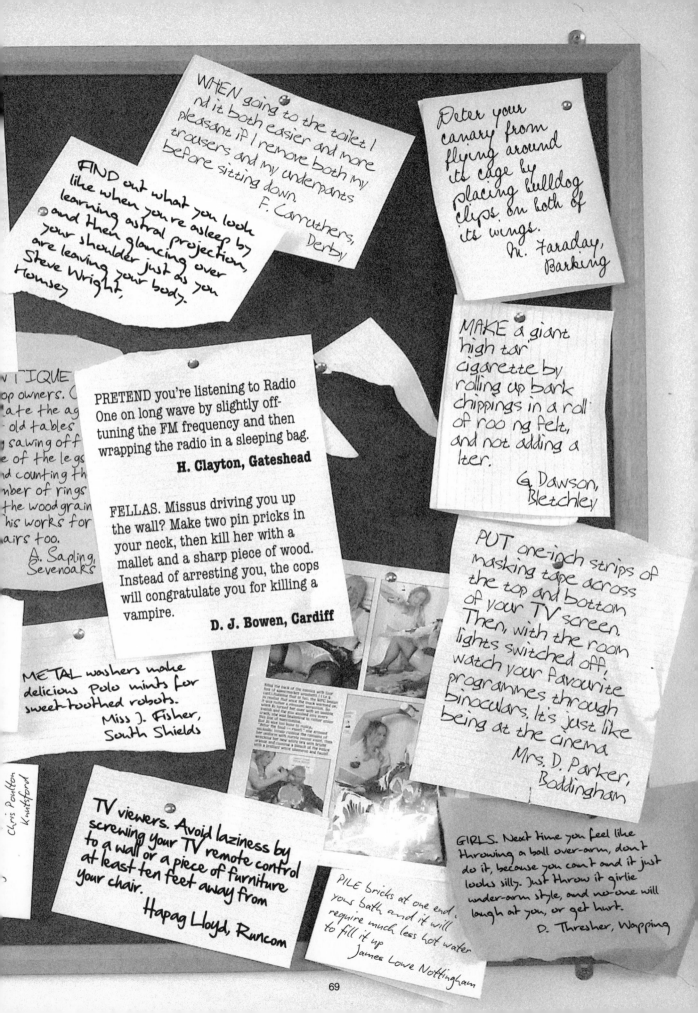

TOP DOG TIPS

DOG owners. Next time your dog does a 'soft one' on the beach annoy metal detector owners by dropping nuts and bolts into it and then covering it with sand.

L. O'Hara, Inverness

BUTCHERS. Make a mockery of the phrase 'as fit as a butcher's dog' by neglecting your dog horribly.

Big Tom, London

SMALL dog owners. Too lazy to take the little fellow out for a walk? Simply place him on a record player turntable and tie his lead to the arm. Set it away at 33 rpm for a gentle stroll, 45 rpm for a good walk and 78 rpm for a jog.

John Stormont, e-mail

BUSY executives. Don't buy a Dachshund. Their amusing sausage shape means they take 50% longer to stroke than other dogs, and time is money.

R Bowen, e-mail

DOG OWNERS. Keep a plastic bag full of excrement behind the kitchen door. When you exercise the dog, take it with you to save collecting a new lot each time.

Phoebe Handrail, Yapton

SPOONERISE Rolf Harris's name. Hey Presto! You're saying it in a dog's voice.

Mr C., e-mail

DOG LOVERS. Reduce your chances of going blind by only buying brown or black labradors.

Ian E., Glasgow

DOG owners. Next time your mutt bites the postman's arse, make sure you say "well, he's never done that before."

Stu Perry the Postie, Isle of Man

DOG owners. Don't waste money on a lead. Simply walk your dog backwards holding its tail.

Shauny Boy, e-mail

DOG OWNERS. Never lose your TV remote control again. Simply sellotape it to the back of your dog, and hey presto!

Whistle, and the device is at your beck and call! This can also apply to hot drinks, after intense training.

Theodore Tramp, e-mail

DOG owners. Avoid getting fined for failing to clean up after your pooch by carrying a joke shop dog poo around with you in a transparent polythene bag when you walk your pet.

Mark Anderson, Coventry

AVOID dogs molesting your leg under the dinner table by coating your trousers below the knee with Ralgex or Fiery Jack.

Neil Fortune, e-mail

SAVE money on expensive hole punches by goading a Great Dane into snapping at you while you slip the appropriate documents between its foaming canines. It may help to make a pencil mark halfway along the edge, and try to line this up with the cleft in the dog's top lip.

Mike Fitzgerald, Jersey

DOG owners. Stop your pet drooling whenever you fry bacon by placing an odour-eater under each rasher as it cooks.

L. Marrion, Gloucester

PREVENT your dog from feeling left out at breakfast time by feeding him dog food out of a 'Variety Pack'-size Cornflakes packet.

D. Pumell, Bristol

TIRED of being nagged to walk the dog? Pretend you've already taken it out by unrolling a turkey rasher out the side of its mouth whilst it lies by the fire to give it that shagged out look.

D. Pickering, Whitehaven

CIRCUMCISE your randy dog by attaching sandpaper 'chaps' to the bottom of your trouser legs.

R.T., Garston

MIX luminous paint with your dog food to help prevent unfortunate pedestrians treading in dog mess during the dark winter evenings.

Simon Mellishoe, Redhill

A ROLLER skate painted yellow and with the wheels removed makes a handy 'foot clamp' for anyone standing in your garden without permission.

*Mrs M.,
Burn Catton*

GIRLS. Stuff a pitta bread with tampons, lipstick, etc. Your friends will be green with envy at your 'Viviene Westwood'-style clutch bag.

*Bunny McMahon,
Cork*

each film at a time, but not really paying attention to any of them. Then, at midnight, nip into a nearby adult cinema to watch ten minutes of a third rate porn movie before going home to bed.

*P. Croft,
Blyth*

AVOID cut fingers when chopping vegetables by getting someone else to hold the vegetables for you while you simply chop away.

*I. J. Alexander,
Birmingham*

WEEDY fellas. Develop a right arm like Arnold Schwarzenegger in a matter of weeks by investing in the latest workout video by Cindy Crawford.

*B. Beater,
St Annes*

WHILST dieting, I used to weigh myself each week. The difference between successive weights was the amount that I had either gained or lost.

*A. J. Marsh,
Tongharn, Surrey*

SAVE time and hot water in the mornings by simply popping your cold, damp facecloth into the microwave.

*P. Wilson,
Troon*

MAKE bathtime as much fun for kiddies as a trip to the seaside by chucking a bucket of sand, a bag of salt, a dog turd and a broken bottle into the bath with them.

*Archie Hitch,
Merton*

BAKERS and coffee shop owners. Encourage your customers to buy by having the smell of a newly built house in your establishment.

D. Hull, Hull

OBTAIN the effects of satellite TV by nailing a dustbin lid to the front of your house, then filling an old fish tank with shit and sitting, staring at it for 23 hours a day.

*J. Brush,
Loughborough*

TAKE a lead out of the skateboarders' book this winter. Strap egg cartons to your knees and elbows to prevent injury when falling on icy pavements.

*G. Hall,
Motherwell*

RE-CREATE the effect of watching satellite television by going to a multi-screen movie complex and walking to and fro between cinemas watching two minutes of

A SIMPLE car theft prevention technique can be put to effective use on houses too. Have your house number engraved on your front window. Would-be thieves will then think twice before breaking in.

*J. Begley,
Timperley*

HAVING problems removing your children's heads from iron railings? No need to call the Fire Brigade. Simply pop a lubricated condom on each of the child's ears, and gently pull them free.

*Mr N. Roast,
Aberness*

ALWAYS divide the number of pages in a book by the price to see whether or not it represents good value for money. Compare different books before deciding which to buy.

*L. Flashing,
Andover*

STEEL wool moistened with a drop of baby oil is ideal for wiping baby robots' bottoms with.

*J. T.,
Northumberland*

CHICORY TIPS

SMOKERS. Wear a golf visor between your nose and top lip to keep your cigarette dry in the shower.

**D. Quigley,
Rotherham**

WHEN buying a camera, always buy a second one so that if you sell the first you will be able to take a picture of it for advertising purposes.

**A. Harmer,
Frodsham**

RAMBLERS. In the countryside leaving gates open will help the farmer, as he will not have to climb down from his tractor.

**W. A. Pratt,
London**

A RED balloon, full of petrol, tied to the end of a broom shank would make a perfect fairytale giant's match.

**G. Dawson,
Bletchley**

SAVE all the time and effort involved in playing fruit machines by simply sending all your money to the fruit machine manufacturers together with a note asking them to send 70% of it back to you.

**G. Hawkins,
Brighton**

FATTIES. Pay someone to walk behind you, juggling, swallowing swords or eating fire, etc. This will divert attention from your obesity.

**R. Warren,
Teddington**

WASHING up bottles, once empty, make ideal containers for storing petrol. I always buy a few gallons if I see a special offer anywhere, and keep it under the stairs or on top of my wardrobe.

**Mrs S. Gray,
Carlisle**

FARMERS. Get butter out of your cows by 'rodeo riding' them for an hour or two before milking time.

**Volker Holz,
Fuerth, Germany**

NAIL old floorboards to your tree in order to attract woodpeckers.

**Robin Pearce,
Southampton**

GET extra shine from your light bulbs without even changing them. Simply rewire them with thicker flex, thus allowing much more electricity into the bulb.

**K. Black,
Alnwick**

HAVING trouble with obscene phone callers? Try installing an answering machine, and then not switching it on.

**A. Dawson,
Liverpool**

WEIGH toilet rolls on your kitchen scales and record their weight after each visit to the toilet. On each occasion deduct the new weight from their previous weight. The figure remaining will be the exact weight of toilet tissue which you have used on that particular 'visit'.

**Mrs Howard,
Bingley**

BOOKIES. Increase your profits by not giving customers 'clues' in the form of odds as to which horse will win a race
Den Haag, Holland

AVOID sky high electricity bills, a dry, stuffy house and stained walls by telling the electricity company to stuff their electric central heating up their arses.
T. Wicks, Rilham

LADIES. Check both your breasts are the same size by making a plaster mould of each. Fill both moulds with water, then pour the contents into two separate measuring jugs. The amounts of water in each will tell you which 'jug' is the bigger.
Mr S. Brown, Peckenham

HELP forget the farce that was Prince Andrew's marriage by sticking the head of your favourite film actress over Fergie's head on any souvenirs you have around the house. I now have an attractive portrait of Prince Andrew with Hollywood stunner Michelle Pfeiffer on my mantlepiece.
Mrs Dawn Potts, Cheltenham

SAVE pounds at Christmas by not sending cards or presents to elderly relatives whose marbles have probably gone anyway and who wouldn't know you from Adam.
B. Peacock, Swindon

IF YOU foul the air in someone else's bathroom, disguise the smell by lighting a match and setting fire to the hand towel.
Mrs D. Parkinson, Billericay

AS adverts on the television tell us not to use light switches if we smell gas, I find it useful to always have a candle ready for use in such emergencies.
Mrs D. Bibby, Rugby

IMPRESS friends with your knowledge of country ways when out walking by stopping suddenly, sniffing loudly once or twice, then hissing "Fox. Can you smell it?" under your breath. Repeat with badger, deer etc.
Andrew Wedderburn, Windermere

PREVENT eggs from rolling off kitchen work surfaces by placing them on a small dollop of black treacle.
L. Bowman, Tijuana

CONVERT any old hat to a smart 'Sherlock Holmes'-style deerstalker by draping a pair of socks down over your ears before donning it. Remember to catch the socks when your hat is doffed.
Robert Stetson, Jedburgh

FED UP with fast food restaurants? Empty a tin of vegetable soup on their doorstep. It'll look like one of their customers has thrown up.
Scott Shaw, Hemel Hempstead

DRILL a one inch diameter hole in your refrigerator door. This will allow you to check that the light goes off when the door is closed.
T. Baccus, Cheltenham

DISCARDED cigarette butts make economical and efficient ear plugs and also reduce the levels of nicotine entering your ears as a result of passive smoking.
Simon Handley, Edinburgh

PARENTS. Baffle everyone your baby daughter will ever meet by calling her 'Shivorn' but insist it is pronounced 'Sea O'Ban'.
A. Delarosa, Hove

WHILE out shopping, remove the batteries from any clocks or other battery-operated appliances around the house, and replace them when you return home. This will result in a considerable saving in electricity over a long period of time.
Mrs D. Bibby, Rugby

Geoff Capes's budgie

James, Hunt's Motoring Tips

ALWAYS flash your hazard warning lights, or stick a raised thumb out of the window after forcing your way into a flow of fast moving traffic. This friendly gesture will ensure that the driver behind you quickly forgets the emergency stop you caused him to make, and will more than make up for any rear end collision damage he has suffered from the car behind.

David Connor, Chingford

MOTORISTS. Stick a cardboard cut-out ear to the back of your mobile phone. That way, when using the phone whilst driving, it will look like you are fiddling with your ear, which is not illegal.

Andrew Laurence, e-mail

DRINK drivers. Before motoring home after an evening on the piss, try sucking on an extra strong mint. Later, when police stop you for swerving around in the middle of the road and failing to stop at a red light, they'll never in a million years suspect you've been drinking.

R. Luck, H. M. Prison, Shotts

MOTORISTS. Park for free in any city centre by smashing the windows, pulling out the radio and attaching a 'Police Aware' sticker to the front windscreen of your car. Long term parkers may wish to burn their vehicles out for greater effect.

Rob Chingford, e-mail

FOOL other drivers into thinking you have an expensive car phone by holding an old TV or video remote control up to your ear and occasionally swerving across the road and mounting the kerb.

Mike Penny, Coventry

DRUNKEN drivers. When making your way home from a night out, put 'L' plates on your car to convince patrolling police that any careless driving is the result of inexperience rather than drink. How you explain a 3am driving lesson is up to you.

Captain Fuck, Derrington

WHEN on the continent, simplify the process of driving on the 'wrong' side of the road by placing your rear view mirror above your back windscreen. Then simply look over your shoulder whilst driving and view the road ahead in the re-positioned mirror. Everything will appear perfectly normal, with cars driving on the 'proper' side of the road.

J. Sulzer, Ipswich

WINTER is the time to freeze petrol and store it in the ice tray of your fridge. Come summer these handy 'petrol cubes' will help to cool your engine as you drive along.

B. Baxter, Potters Bar

PENSIONERS. Try sitting on a pile of encyclopedias next time you go for a drive in your car. That way you'll be able to see out of the front window.

B. Flynn, Burnley

AND while you're on, try pushing the pedal on the right down towards the floor. That will make your car move forwards more quickly.

B. Flynn, Burnley

TAXI drivers. Why not pop into the garage and ask them to fix your indicator lights for you so that other motorists know where the fuck you are going.

E. Murphy, Ipswich

FOOL onlookers into believing your car has central locking by leaving all the doors unlocked except the driver's door. When you return open the driver's door and - hey presto! All the doors are suddenly unlocked.

Tom Bradley, Heaton

PARKING problems? Tie a balloon to the front bumper of your car, and Sellotape a drawing pin to the rear wall of your garage. When you hear the balloon burst, apply the brakes.

Q. Quicksave, Quebec

CENTRALLY position your car within your garage by fixing a torch to the exact centre of the bonnet. Then line up the beam with a target placed on the centre of the rear wall (above the drawing pin). Then drive slowly forwards, aiming the beam at the target (until the balloon bursts).

Q. Quicksave, Quebec

ATTACH a Christmas cracker by two pieces of string, one to your front bumper and one to your garage wall, the total length being equal to that of your garage. Then reverse your car out the garage. When the cracker explodes, stop, get out of the car, and close the garage door.

Q. Quicksave, Quebec

ROAD rage drivers. Settle your dispute honourably by removing your car aerials and having a fencing duel. The aerials will retract if they hit a solid object, thus preventing serious injury.

Pete Doolan, Yeovil

HEARSE drivers. Try attaching flashing yellow lights to your roof, the way that other slow-moving vehicles do. I don't wish to appear disrespectful, but I'm sure grieving relatives would find a few flashing lights a lot more dignified than a car skidding into the back of the deceased sending the coffin flying out through the front windscreen.

A. Rayleigh, Sidcup

MOTORISTS. Always have a hot pie in your hands in heavy traffic. Each time the traffic grinds to a halt, just reach for the pie. The instant you place it to your lips the traffic begins to move. This works especially well with the molten lava apple turnovers from KFC.

Pat Jackson, e-mail

BOY racers. Give your car that lowered-suspension, ground-hugging racing look by driving around with 12 paving slabs in the boot and a bag of builders' sand under each front seat.

James Augustini, Leicester

PRESSING the middle pedal in my car helps me to slow down when approaching busy junctions or built-up areas.

Mr G. Lane, Cleveland

LEAVE your sidelights on all day to make distant oncoming drivers think you might be driving a Volvo.

P. Delaney, Dublin

MOTORISTS. When asking for directions from a woman always look for one with small tits as they've usually got more brains. God seldom gives them both.

G. Kiss, Crawley

AN OLD spectacle lens makes an ideal and easily fitted 'sunroof' for a tortoise.

J. Dodger, Milton Keynes

A WIRE brush makes an ideal bed of nails for a hamster.

John Tait, Thropton

FELLAS. Next time you have to wrap up a present, don't, because you're shite at it. Give it to the wife and she'll do it properly with extra girlie bows and fiddly bits while you're down the pub.

Daphnie Treloar, Cardiff

NEVER lunge at an escaped parrot or budgie in an attempt to capture him. Simply hold out a walking stick in front of him and he will 'hop' onto it. Then return him gently to his cage.

Linda Howarth, Manchester

GIVE your pet tortoise protective 'bull bars' by slipping the wire off a champagne cork over his head.

J. Bobble, Tinsley

WIG wearers. Secure your toupee in high winds by wearing a brightly coloured party hat with an elasticated chin strap. Carry a balloon and a bottle of wine, and you'll pass off as an innocent party-goer.

N. Lost, Sorryford

GET your girlfriend to suck a Steradent tablet whilst giving you a blowjob. Not only will it give her a dazzling smile, your bell-end will come out Bristol fashion!

J. T., Thropton

WHEN standing on a chair to change a light bulb, always put the chair into position below the light before standing on it. It becomes much harder to move the chair once you are standing on it.

T. Macroadstone, Derby

PRETEND to live in a hard water area by placing finely ground pieces of egg shell in the bottom of your kettle.

A. J. Hill, Grantham, Hull

MUMS. Fit an extra handle onto your pram so that it can be pushed either way.

Mike Howarth, Manchester

AVOID the unnecessary expense of buying clay pigeons by shooting real ones.

A. Smith, Rosyth

BELL RINGERS. Don't waste time raising money to save your church bells. Get the same teeth-grating effect by simply dropping different lengths of scaffolding pipe off the roof of the church at 8 o'clock every Sunday morning.

Mark Smith, Wantage

IF you get to the supermarket checkout only to find that you have left your purse at home, avoid embarrassment by pretending to have a nose bleed. Invariably one of the assistants will help you to the lavatory where you can remain until the store has closed.

Mrs F. Anglia, Anglia

MEN. Make women think you are a good lover by cutting scratches in your back with a fork before walking shirtless along the beach.

Les Washington, Camberley

MALTESERS make ideal packing material for fragile objects being sent through the post. And the recipient can of course eat them without putting on weight.

R. B., Chelsea

TWO pieces of macaroni stuck together would make an ideal pair of binoculars for any little gingerbread men who express an interest in ornithology.

Mrs L. H., Longhorsely

OLD shoelaces should never be thrown away. Soak them overnight in petrol, roll them in lard, then pop them in the fridge for a few hours. Hey presto. Perfect candles.

Rose Gray, Godalming

AVOID the frustration of repeatedly losing your TV remote control by keeping it in a 'cowboy'-style holster fashioned out of a child's sock and an old belt.

M. Thornton, Jesmond

CREATE the impression of bats in your attic by pinning used 'one cup' tea bags by their strings to the roof beams.

K. Newton, Burnley

FAT people. Keep your hands warm in winter by unbuttoning your shirt and tucking them in between the rolling layers of fat on your belly.

M. Jackson, Wolverhampton

FOOL next door neighbours into thinking you have more stairs than them by banging your feet twice on each step.

C. B., Sedgefield

SAVE time when making a cup of tea by pre-heating the water in a saucepan before putting it in the kettle.

Susan Craven, Leeds

DON'T waste any money on over-priced toilet fresheners. Simply hang pleasant-smelling herbal tea bags over the rim of the loo, and every time you flush, hey presto! Your toilet will fill up with lovely tea.

A. Asda, Castleton

MAKE your own 'glitter' this Christmas by wrapping grains of sugar in kitchen foil.

Mr T. Tunnel, Jarrow

A LENGTH of drainpipe with a roller skate fastened to each end makes an ideal 'car' for a snake.

L. Hall, Morpeth

PAN'S PEOPLE

Dr. Who'se Top Tip Tardis

GIVE your house that 'city centre car park' feel by putting 'P' and 'NO SPACES' signs on the front door, and inviting tramps in to urinate down your stairs.

D. U.,
Hong Kong

DON'T throw away that old dart. Once removed, the flight makes four excellent feathers for use in conjunction with spare hat bands.

Mrs J. Tapioca,
Wivenhoe

TOWNIES. Whenever you see country folk driving into town in their green Range Rovers to go shopping, jump up and down screaming 'Get off my land!' Then shoot their dog.

Y. Pages,
Cheshire

CONVINCE dinner guests that your wife has a tapeworm by teaching her to regurgitate noodles while you hold a spoonful of sugar to her mouth.

Mr D. Light-Infantry,
Gateshead

YOUNG mothers. Pretend to be unbelievably dull and unimaginative by meeting other young mothers in public places and only ever talking about your children.

Phil Telfer,
e-mail

BRIGHTEN up breakfasttime by making your toast into simple but effective 'Maltese Cross' shapes by nibbling out an identical section from each of the four corners.

J. Hudson,
Mitcham

POLO mints make ideal 'life belts' for earwigs. Except they they don't float. And they dissolve in water.

A. E. Greenall,
Liverpool

WHEN attacked by a large polar bear, roll into a ball and remain perfectly still. Any movement on your part will excite the animal and increase your chance of injury.

Mrs B. Sellers,
Cricklewood

PUT a stop to car thieves by syphoning off all your petrol whenever you park your car, and carrying it round with you in one or two plastic buckets.

D. Griffiths,
Kent

A DIGESTIVE biscuit topped with tomato ketchup and a slice of processed cheese makes a popular 'mini pizza' for kid's parties.

Mrs J. Crooks,
Grantham

CAR thieves. Always carry a spare can of petrol with you in case the driver has syphoned off all the petrol from his car and is carrying it round with him in one or two plastic buckets.

A. Thief,
Kent

AT WEDDINGS ask the bride or groom to wear a sandwich board with their names, the date and the name of the church etc. written on it in bold letters.

Ken Road,
Luton

CONFUSE your milkman by ordering one pint of milk each day, then buying a dozen extra pints from a nearby shop, thus leaving thirteen empty bottles on the doorstep the following morning. Add to his confusion by leaving a lighted candle in every other bottle.

Mrs P. Wilkinson,
Hemel Hempstead

TREAT yourself on birthdays or other special occasions by carrying your favourite comfortable chair around with you everywhere you go. When you get tired of carrying the chair you can sit down in it and give yourself a well earned rest.

Gary Bennett,
Oxford

TAKE a leaking tin of red paint to your local D.I.Y. superstore, carry it into the shop and demand a refund. Then return straight to your car in the crowded car park by simply following the trail of paint.

R. Hiles,
Edinburgh

MAKE your own teabags by pouring tea into an After Eight mint envelope, and then stapling it closed along the top edge, before puncturing the sides two thousand times with a pin.

A. Asda,
Castleford

RENEW the bottom of an old bucket by placing it on the kitchen table and drawing a line around the base. Cut out the circle and press it hard into the bottom of the bucket.

Mike Howarth,
Manchester

HOUSEWIVES. Brighten up Mondays by coating your kitchen floor with 'Quavers' in order to recreate the sound of walking through virgin snow whilst preparing the tea.

Mrs T.,
Thropton

CREATE instant designer stubble by sucking a magnet and dipping your chin in a bowl of iron filings.

B. Vilbins,
Birmingham

CONFUSE shopkeepers by buying a sheet of wrapping paper and asking them to wrap it.

D. Treloar,
Wandsworth

The
Black & White
MINSTRELS
Black & White
TIPS

BY making a simple periscope out of toilet roll tubes and the lenses from an old pair of reflective sunglasses, it is possible to watch your TV from beneath your floorboards.

P. N. Thorne,
Bristol

IF your brakes fail whilst reversing, open all your car doors, and if possible the boot. Similarly, these will greatly increase wind resistance and help bring the vehicle to a standstill.

V. Ground,
Hartlepool

SLIMMERS. Use sand in coffee instead of sugar. Not only is it free, and contains no calories, but it can also be used more than once, as it doesn't dissolve.

P. Crocker,
Devon

TWO buttered pieces of bread put together with a piece of cheese in between makes an exciting lunchtime snack. This tasty treat is now a regular in my household. My wife Jean calls it 'Jack's Cheese and Bread Snack'.

Mr J. Pewty,
Leeds

STEAL money from flat-mates by borrowing £5 then moving to Fife. (If you live in Fife, move to South Fife.)

Anon,
Fife

SEAGULLS. Fly upside down next time you're over Cornwall. I can assure you it isn't even worth shitting on.

I. Ashenden,
Falmouth

SAVE the expense of buying a plastic 'red nose' on Comic Relief day by simply drinking heavily for years on end until your own nose becomes red and swollen.

I.P. Head,
Middlesbrough

AGORAPHOBICS. Feel more comfortable in large open spaces by looking the right way through a pair of binoculars.

T. R. Ilbey,
Hattington

HITCHCOCK fans. Offer to make your wife a sandwich, then drill a hole in the bedroom wall and watch her getting into the shower.

P. Todrie,
Aberdeen

A LARGE sheet of polystyrene placed on your car roof and trimmed to shape makes an ideal 'all weather' snow covering with which to baffle fellow motorists in summer.

Steve Murphy, Gloucester

HOUSE guests will think your fingernails grow quickly if you cut up a table tennis ball and sprinkle pieces around your bathroom sink every morning.

F. Foster, Froddingham

RUN out of ice for party drinks? Frozen peas are an ideal replacement, and can always be washed and re-used afterwards.

D. Pumell, Bristol

A TREBOR soft mint and child's paint brush make an ideal curling stone and brush for gerbil 'Highland Games'.

A. E. G., Liverpool

PREVENT your milkman from becoming complacent by never ordering the same number of pints twice, and hiding your empties all around your front garden.

M. Cooper, Leyland

AVOID losing contact lenses by drilling a small hole in each one and connecting them with a length of nylon fishing line. This can then be worn around the neck.

B. Morgan, Criccieth

PROLONG the life of leather underpants by spraying them with 'Scotch Guard' before use.

N. Thorpe, Hockley

SHOPKEEPERS. Reduce shoplifting by banning third rate television celebrities from your shop.

A. Price, Worthing

INJECT food colouring into the bottom of your toothpaste tube using a hypodermic needle. When the toothpaste begins to appear coloured, you'll know it's time to buy a new tube.

G. Ducksworth, Bamsley

FOOL distant corner shop owners into thinking that you live nearby simply by driving for miles to make frequent early morning and late evening visits to their shop to buy cigarettes, milk, bread and other groceries.

M. Renshaw, London

ALWAYS carry a five pence piece in your pocket so that if you fancy a Chinese takeaway you can buy a plastic fork.

H. Attwell, Enfield

DON'T fork out on expensive smoke alarms. Simply fill balloons with water and hang them from the ceiling. Then cover the floor with air-filled balloons, each with a drawing pin stuck to the top. In the event of a fire the temperature will cause the air-filled balloons to rise up from the floor, and the pins will burst the water-filled balloons, thus extinguishing the fire. Probably.

D. P., Wiltshire

MAKE everyone think you wear glasses by making a mark on the bridge of your nose with a hot teaspoon every morning.

Morris Minor, Coventry

SMOKING after sex is much easier if you use a metal funnel as a cigarette holder. Insert the cigarette inside the funnel so that the funnel acts as an ashtray whilst you lie on your back. To tip the ash, simply nod your head a couple of times.

H. Higson, Lincoln

CARAVAN owners planning to use the A5 between Betwys-y-Coed and Llangollen on the first day of Easter bank holiday next year, please stay at home. I'm visiting my girlfriend that day and I can't afford to be 7 hours late.

P. Bandwagon, Clywd

It's a Bug's Life

MOTHS dipped in lighter fuel and released into a room lit by candles suspended from the ceiling make an effective and inexpensive indoor firework display.

Mike Y., e-mail

GIVE house spiders a taste of their own medicine by applying a coat of spray-mount to all the surfaces in your home.

Felixthehat, e-mail

CYCLISTS. Avoid getting flies in your eyes by making an improvised pair of goggles out of two tea strainers.

P. Presto, Preston

STOP being scared of spiders by handling spiders on a regular basis until you aren't scared of spiders anymore.

Mrs Nan Chester, Manchester

CHEESE slices cut up into small, stamp-sized rectangles make ideal yoga mats for flies.

Jake Parsons, Middlesbrough

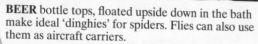

BEER bottle tops, floated upside down in the bath make ideal 'dinghies' for spiders. Flies can also use them as aircraft carriers.

M. Harwood, Yeadon

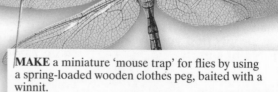

MAKE a miniature 'mouse trap' for flies by using a spring-loaded wooden clothes peg, baited with a winnit.

T. Hawthorns, West Bromwich

TRICK spiders into thinking they have caught a fly by flicking cigarette ash into their cobwebs.
Andy Woolfoot, Cirencester

A SPIDER painted green makes an excellent leafy bit for the top of a tomato.
B. Wright, Castleford

REVIVE dying moths by placing them on a small droplet of sugary water.
C. Coup, Basildon

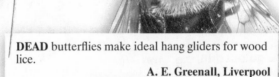

DEAD butterflies make ideal hang gliders for wood lice.
A. E. Greenall, Liverpool

SHAPE rusty iron filings into dog turds. When flies eat it they will be too heavy to take off and can be easily caught with a magnet.
Paul Kelly, Wimbledon

PREVENT bees and butterflies stealing your pollen by enclosing each flower head in a plastic bag securely fastened around the stem with a clothes peg.
P. Reaney, Rothwell

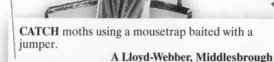

CATCH moths using a mousetrap baited with a jumper.
A Lloyd-Webber, Middlesbrough

VETS. A human armpit hair makes a great prosthetic leg for an invalid spider.
Hedgepig, Crewe

THE MANY FACES OF
MIKE YARWOOD

Oooh, Betty.
(Frank Spencer)

TAKE a tip from Frankenstein. Before you go out drinking, tape a small battery to your cock. The tiny electrical charge will be enough to keep it stimulated, and no matter how much you drink you'll be 'Ever Ready' for sex.

M. Shelley, Ipswich

RE-CREATE the fairground thrills of the Waltzer in your own home by simply drinking 12 cans of Carlsberg

And this is me. (Mike Yarwood)

Special Brew then asking a couple of friends to stand at the end of your bed and occasionally give it a violent shove as you try to get to sleep.

S. Leone, Moffat

MAKE your own extra large matches by soaking a glacier cherry in petrol then sticking it on the end of a wooden lollipop stick.

G. Dawson, Bletchley

WHEN buying fruit by the pound, buy grapes instead of apples. Apples are much heavier.

Edna Thompson, Bishopsgate

ENSURE circular objects such as vases stand centrally on your mantlepiece by subtracting the diameter of the object from the length of the mantlepiece and dividing by two. Then simply cut a piece of string to that length. Get a friend to hold one end of the string flush to one side of the mantlepiece, and then slide the vase or object along the length of the string towards the centre of the mantlepiece. Stop only when the string runs out, and its other end abuts the base of the vase or object. The string can then be popped into the vase, and used again later should the ornament be moved for any reason.

M. Moleson, Wadebridge

MAKE motorists sweat for up to ten days. Sit inside a cardboard box on top of a stick at the side of the road and take a flash photo of every car as it goes by.

Alan Currie, Wylam

MUMS over 50. Don't forget the last date for boiling Christmas carrots and sprouts is the 5th December.

Pete O'Bog, West Bromwich

GET rid of bats by attaching mouse traps to helium-filled balloons and releasing them at night.

B. Newton, Liverpool

SPECTACLE wearers. Enjoy foreign language films without the bothersome subtitles by sticking a strip of brown parcel tape across the lower half of your lenses.

J. Lofts, Chiswick

SAVE a fortune on laundry bills. Give your dirty shirts to Oxfam. They will wash and iron them and you can then buy them back for 50 pence.

J. B. Cartland, Brighton

Silly Billy.
(Denis Healey)

SATELLITE TV bosses. Save a fortune in broadcasting costs by switching off the Adult Channel at five past midnight. There's no point in broadcasting the remaining 3 hours and 55 minutes of porn. After five minutes all your viewers have already lost their mess, switched off and gone to bed.

Mr Highbury, Woolwich

84

TOP TIPPLES

FELLAS. Avoid pulling ugly birds. Simply drink 14 pints of beer and hey presto! Everyone you chat up looks like Catherine Zeta Jones.
Paul & Scotty, BFPO 544 DRS

MAKE sure she's still a stunner the next morning by hiding a bottle of vodka under your pillow, and drinking it before she wakes up. Hey presto! Breakfast with Cindy Crawford.
Paul & Scotty, BFPO 544 DRS

A DROP of whisky rubbed regularly into woodworm-infected furniture will make the woodworms too drunk to have sex, and therefore unable to reproduce.
N.M., Anfield Plain

POPPING two 'Alka Seltzer' tablets into a newly-opened can of beer has exactly the same effect as a 'widget', and has the added advantage of preventing hangovers.
C. Atkinson, Windsor

ADD beer to washing-up liquid to change it from lem-on flavour to shandy flavour.
Dave Patterson, Bournemouth

DRINKERS. Don't waste valuable time stopping to eat. Simply place a sausage end-up in your pint, then each time you take a sip, you can take a bite of your meaty beer-marinated treat.
Jamie Nedved, e-mail

ENSURE a good night's sleep by knocking back a large bottle of gin before retiring to bed.
T. Horswill, Bedford

SMUGGLE whisky out of the house by pouring it down the sink and collecting it in a saucepan under the drainpipe.
Steven Pearlman, Soapdish, Hants.

PUTTING just the right amount of gin in your goldfish bowl makes the fishes' eyes bulge and causes them to swim in an amusing manner.
Magnus McIntyre, Oxford

SAVE on booze by drinking cold tea instead of whisky. The following morning you can create the effects of a hangover by drinking a thimble full of washing-up liquid and banging your head repeatedly on a wall.
F. Horton, Chipping Norton

MAKE the man in the off licence think you're a doctor by going in early every morning carrying your small leather bag and buying a large bottle of gin.
P.C., Leicester

BRIGHTEN up dull Monday mornings at work by concealing a bottle of vodka in your jacket pocket and taking swigs from it at regular intervals throughout the day.
T. Horswill, Bedford

ALCOHOLICS. Increase the strength of your booze by an eighth by giving a pint of blood immediately before going on a bender.
Lionel Peppercorn, e-mail

AMATEUR winemakers. Pretend you tread your own grapes by standing in a bowl of purple rinse hair dye.
Dave Eccleston, Huyton

OLYMPIC athletes. Conceal the fact that you have taken performance-enhancing drugs by simply running a little bit slower and letting someone else win.

A. Plasticman,
London

VICARS. Raise much-needed restoration funds by inviting the owners of lost pets to climb to the top of your steeple in order to look for their missing animals, in return for a small donation.

B. O. Nails,
Nantwich

A WIRE paperclip, carefully unfolded, is ideal for picking up small pieces of cheese, pineapple chunks or cocktail sausages.

S. Jones,
Edinburgh

MAKE edible jumpers for gingerbread men by simply 'knitting' spaghetti with chop sticks.

Mrs L.H.,
Longhorsely

FED up with oral sex? Stop your bird from giving you blowjobs by marrying her.

M.A.,
Leeds

SET UP a Haagen Dazs ice cream franchise next door to your local Weight Watchers clinic. Give away freebies to slim people and watch the fat fuckers squirm.

D. R.,
Croydon

CUT laundry bills. Tie your dirty linen to your neighbour's roof rack next time he visits the car wash.

R. Hughes,
Mid Glamorgan

FETE organisers. Put a copy of the Reader's Digest on your tombola stall. Then write to them saying that THEY have been entered in YOUR prize draw.

T. Snaith,
Blyth

STICKING two black circles in the top corners of your TV screen makes the newsreaders look like Mickey Mouse.

S. Teardrop,
Teddlebranbuds

A PAIR of fox terriers, one strapped to each foot, make ideal 'organic' rollerskates.

Justin Deegan,
Victoria, Australia

POP TARTS make ideal radiators for dolls' houses.

N. Stiles,
Stockport

GIVE yourself an Elvis-style lip by knotting a piece of cotton thread and lodging it between your two front teeth, pulling it tight and then wrapping the other end several times around your ear.

B. Idol,
Hollywood

IF YOU want to know the time during Baywatch, remember to put your wristwatch on the other hand.

P. Green,
Wakefield

MAKE it look like your car smokes by sticking a roll of white paper in the exhaust pipe. Simple.

Stephen Dunn,
Lilishaw

SHOE segs make ideal 'fridge magnets' for use on wooden cupboards etc.

D. B.,
Harwich

FOOL people into thinking you are an octopus by drinking several litres of ink and farting everytime someone startles you.

D. Grear, e-mail

TAKE a tip from bank robbers. Leave your engine running when going into a shop to buy frozen vegetables. Making a 'quick getaway' will reduce the risk of them thawing before you get home.

Mrs G. Walton,
Holmfirth

MOTORCYCLISTS. Save cigarette filters and stick them up your nostrils. These will prevent dirt getting in, whilst still allowing you to breathe.

S. Pissuillie,
Mackay, Australia

COP TIPS

DETER burglars by placing a card in your kitchen window which reads 'No Valuables Kept in the House Overnight.'

Glen Atkinson,
e-mail

WHEELIE bins left at the gate make ideal shopping trolleys for burglars.

John Tait,
Thropton

IGNORE advice to leave a light on when you go out, in case of burglars. If anyone is heartless enough to break into your home, they should jolly well be left to find the light switches for themselves. Making things easier for them will only encourage these people to commit more crime.

H. Stevenage,
North'land

WHEN leaving your house empty, nip across into your neighbour's garden and prize open one of their windows. This will make their house a far more attractive proposition to burglars than your own.

Mr G. Woodward,
Gillingham

MOTORISTS. When stopped by the police for speeding or driving dangerously, always indignantly point out that they could better spend their time arresting 'proper' criminals. I haven't tried it myself, but I'm sure they'd see your point and let you off with a warning.

Matt Greatorex,
e-mail

TRAMPS. Avoid being constantly moved on by sleeping outside department stores and telling the police you are simply queuing early for the sales.

J. King,
Prison

SMASH the entire contents of your home with a sledgehammer before going away on holiday. Then any would-be burglars who break in will get a taste of their own medicine.

Mrs Ena Brown,
Wolverhampton

BURGLARS. Spend half an hour in a hot bath before you do your next 'job'. After a good soak the police will never be able to identify your crinkly fingerprints or 'dabs'.

Thora Pee,
Pontefract

AVOID being mugged in the street by walking along behind a policeman, moving your lips and gesturing as if you are engaged in a friendly conversation with him. If he turns round, simply look confused and ask him for directions to a nearby street.

R. Hollins,
Hammersmith

PLACE your Christmas tree in an alcove, bay window or similar recess. After Christmas block it off using empty cornflakes packets to form a partition wall. Come next December, simply pull down the wall, and hey presto! There's your tree, decorations and all.

B. Carpenter,
Huddersfield

COLLECT empty cornflakes packets in a spare bedroom or attic space. Count them after five years, then divide the total by 260. This will give you a rough idea of how many packets you get through in a week.

B. Fitzpatrick,
Wakefield

EMPTY cereal packets make ideal holders for old toilet roll tubes and milk bottle tops which one should never throw away as they are most handy, and have a variety of uses.

Mrs A. Ellis,
Wrexham

DON'T sell that old banger for scrap! Simply paint it white with a big orange stripe down the side, and stick an old cornflakes packet on the roof with 'POLICE' painted on it. Hey presto! The perfect deterrent for burglars.

Ken Illingworth,
Luton

MAKE your own 'Crunchy Nut Corn Flakes' by buying ordinary cornflakes, drizzling them with honey and sprinkling them with chopped almonds.

Tom Atow,
e-mail

SAVE money on expensive CDs by simply cutting circles of cardboard from an empty cornflakes packet and covering them with foil.

Jamie McKenzie,
West Drayton

MAKE your car look like a taxi (from a considerable distance) by Sellotaping a cornflakes packet to the roof.

A. Gallagher,
Runcorn

ALWAYS buy cornflakes packets in twos so that you can use one to top the other one up should the contents have settled during transit.

D. Pumell,
Bristol

BLT's "Hairy" CORN FLAKES

SERVING SUGGESTION

The Hairy Cornflake's
CORNFLAKE PACKET

IT seems such a waste to throw away old toothbrushes. So when one wears out I nip downstairs to the kitchen and pop it inside the cornflakes box. The following morning it makes a great surprise for the kids.

Mrs D. Partington, Clifton

AVOID getting cornflakes or muesli encrusted to your husband's clothes by keeping cereal packets and washing powder boxes in separate kitchen cupboards.

Mrs B. Murdoch, Bedford

AT party time, cornflakes packets make ideal jelly moulds for anyone requiring large rectangular blocks of jelly. Although they do have the disadvantage of not being waterproof.

Mrs E. Norris, Bath

Top Tips

I FIND that an empty cornflakes box filled with small stones or pebbles makes an ideal paperweight or handy doorstopper.

Mrs M., Liverpool

FILL a Shredded Wheat with pink soap and hey presto! An inexpensive 'Brillo pad'.

Mrs B. Parkinson, Harrow

HANG a cornflakes packet on a piece of string in all the doorways of your house. Bumping into the brightly coloured boxes as you pass through will remind you to close the door behind you.

Mrs A. Ellis, Wrexham

A SHREDDED Wheat on a stick makes a great back scrubber for the first couple of seconds of your bath.

Hapag Lloyd, Runcorn

GIRLS! A pair of Variety-size cornflakes packets are ideal for putting fashionable padded shoulders in your blouse.

Mrs. F. Kitching, Southampton

GIVE your bird-box that 'thatched cottage' look by fixing two Shredded Wheat to the roof.

A. E. Greenall, Liverpool L11

SAVE having to buy expensive personalised number plates by simply changing your name to match your existing plate.

Mr. KVL 741Y,
Lincoln

VICARS. Avoid confetti problems in your churchyard by spraying the bride and groom with a light coating of 'spray mount' adhesive before they leave the church. The confetti will then stick to them, and not be left littering the ground.

John Kean,
New Maiden

A SMALL hole cut out of a window will allow your budgie to come and go as it pleases.

C. Press,
Manchester

FARMERS. Don't throw away those old pairs of rubber kitchen gloves. With the ends of the fingers cut off they make ideal sexy 'peep-hole' bras for cows.

K. Newton,
Burnley

MUMS. Underpants with legs sewn up make very good hats. Our teenage daughter must be the envy of all her friends at school wearing a pair which my husband discarded several years ago.

Mrs B.,
London

WHEN speaking on the phone to someone in America, always start a couple of seconds before they finish their sentence. This will avoid pauses due to transatlantic time delays.

D. G.,
Consett

MUMS. When clearing up after children's parties, always burst balloons before throwing them away. This way you use far fewer dustbin liners.

Mrs M. Smith,
Titchfield Common

WHEN arranging kitchen furniture, avoid placing tables or cupboards directly in front of a fridge or oven as they may prevent the fridge or oven doors from opening properly.

T. Barlow,
Chester

TEACH children the value of money by bursting their football. They will then have to work to earn enough money to buy a replacement.

Mr G. Morgan, Finchley

SAVE money on expensive tickets to open air festivals next summer. Simply put up a tent in your own back garden, piss up the side of it, and steal your own shoes.

Simone Glover,
Tottenham N 15

MAKE a kaleidoscope for kids by stretching cling film over the end of a toilet roll tube and dropping a few pieces of broken coloured glass inside. Remember to tell your kids to always point it downwards when looking in the open end.

Mr A. Gemmill,
Nottingham

CUT old dress trousers into 'slices' with garden shears. The resulting cloth rings make an excellent supply of spare hat bands.

Mrs J. Tapioca,
Wivenhoe

FELLAS. Avoid not getting a shag every time you forget your wife's birthday. Simply give her thirty cards all at once, with "Not to be opened until (date and year)" written on the envelopes. After thirty years she'll probably be so old and ugly she won't be worth shagging anyway, so it won't matter if you forget.

H. Foster,
Gloucester

OBTAIN the appearance of mice infestation by making small holes in your skirting boards and scattering a few currants around the floor.

S. Cooper,
Tring

MAN. UNITED fans. Don't waste money on yet another replica team strip. Simply strap a large plastic penis to your forehead. It will then be perfectly obvious to everybody which team you support.

T. Worthington,
Altrincham

MAKE neighbours think you have Norwegian visitors staying by leaving whale bones outside your back door along with your rubbish.
E. M.,
North Shields

A STIFF toothbrush makes an ideal comb for trendy sideburns.
Spencer D. Group,
Wirral

OLD FOLKS. Stay warm and safe this winter by wrapping yourselves in aluminium foil. Not only will this conserve vital body heat, but it will also make you look a bit like 'Robocop', thus going some way towards deterring would-be burglars.
S. Holmes,
York

THE UNDERSEA

KEEP kiddies amused on shopping trips by giving them three wooden balls each and offering a goldfish to the first one who can knock a passer-by's hat off.
Hapag Lloyd,
Runcorn

STRING dipped in tomato sauce makes perfect reusable spaghetti for kids who don't like spaghetti. My kids never touch the stuff, and don't realise I've been serving them up the same bowl of string for over a year now.
Mr Salmon Broccoli-Bake,
Grimsby

MARRIED couples. Avoid damage to doors by attaching a balloon to the top of the door frame before starting a row. When you storm out of the room at the height of the row closing the door gently will have the same dramatic effect as a violent slam, without causing any damage to the door.
O. Stacey,
Essex

RAILWAY commuters. When boarding your train attach a length of rope to the carriage door, and tie the other end firmly around your ankle. In the event of a crash you will be able to find your way out of the wreckage by simply following the rope.
Dave Parsnip,
Altrincham

A LARGE pot of home-made soup is an inexpensive way to feed the family. Make it last longer by eating it with forks.
Mrs K. Littlewood,
Evesham

TIPS OF Jacques Cousteau

PROLONG your sex sessions by inventing excuses to get up and go downstairs every thirty seconds or so (left the gas on, put the cat out, etc.) This way your lovemaking can last all night long.
S. Grey, Mudfastlieghshire

MAKE neighbours think they've seen a snake by squirming around on their lawn in a rolled-up carpet with a fork dangling from your mouth, and making hissing noises.
Tarn Dale, Glasgow

DIRTY CARPETS? Make your own 'Hoover' by fixing door draft excluder brushes to the blades of an old petrol lawn mower.
Sam Brairo, Truro

CUT out problem pages before you throw magazines away and send them to the Samaritans. They will then be able to help if they encounter any similar problems themselves.
S. Coulkton, Sefton

TAKE your dustbin to the supermarket with you so that you can see which items you have recently run out of.
S. Elliot, London

SAVE money by taking the stitching out of old clothing and using it again.
G.T., Newcastle

SUPER-MARKET cashiers. Why not simply have love-bites tattooed on your necks. That way there would never be any danger of you being without one.
E. Banger, Walsall

HATERS of shirt ironing. If you do the fronts, backs and sleeves first, there are only the collars left to do - and they're a piece of piss.
Geoff Barker, Germany

93

BBC **Sport** newsreaders. **Save time by not reporting on the progress of Andy Murray in tennis tournaments. I have yet to meet any member of the public who likes the miserable sod.**

M. Plywood,
Hull

FORMULA **One fans. Recreate the excitement of your favourite sport by threading coloured beads onto a string, pulling it taut and lowering one end. For added authenticity, single beads can be used for practice, qualifying etc.**

Colin Harrison,
Glasgow

CRICKET **spectators. Take a tip from Barry Manilow fans and strike a match every time a run is scored. When the game is over, simply count the number of used matches to reveal the final score.**

Mr U. Biscuits,
Rotherham

F1 AUTHORITIES. **Looking for new ideas to thwart Lewis Hamilton's bid to become World Champion next year? Simply introduce a rule saying that black drivers must start from the back row of the grid. And leave their handbrake on.**

Colin Fibreboard,
Peterborough

EXPERIENCE **the thrills of a skiing holiday without the expense. Simply tape two planks of wood to your feet, sit in your freezer for three hours, then run into a tree as fast as you can.**

M. Jordan,
Wales

GOLFERS. **An ice cream cornet makes an ideal golf tee for use in emergencies.**

A. Simmons,
Cheltenham

LANDLORDS. **Save thousands of pounds paying hugely-inflated monthly rates for Sky Sports by simply painting a small white pint glass with Tippex in the bottom right-hand corner of your TV screen.**

Ross Bill,
e-mail

SKIERS. **Carry a dog biscuit in your pocket. That way, in the event of an avalanche, the rescue dog will find you first.**

J. Tull,
e-mail

GOLFERS. **Why waste a fortune on expensive covers for the heads of your golf clubs? An empty crisp packet will do the job just as well. Use different flavours for different clubs, e.g. cheese 'n' onion - three iron, salt'n'vinegar - sand wedge, etc.**

A. Simmons,
Cheltenham

WIMBLEDON **tennis organisers. Why not play the finals on the first day of the championships instead of the last? That way the grass will all be green and the players will have a decent surface on which to display their undoubted talents.**

Laurie Penfold,
Sheffield

WORLD

DICKIE